The Strengths Profile Book

Finding What You
Can Do + Love To Do
And Why It Matters

ALEX LINLEY   TRUDY BATEMAN

CAPP PRESS

2018

The Strengths Profile Book

Finding What You Can Do + Love To Do And Why It Matters

Alex Linley

Trudy Bateman

CAPP PRESS

2230-2235 Regents Court, The Crescent, Birmingham Business Park, B37 7YE, United Kingdom

Tel: +44 (0)121 726 5900

capp@capp.co   www.capp.co

enquiries@strengthsprofile.com   www.strengthsprofile.com

Capp Press is a trading name of Capp & Co Ltd, registered in England and Wales, company number 06802155

First published in the United Kingdom in 2010

Second edition published in the United Kingdom in 2018 v2.1

© Capp Press 2018

ISBN: 978-1-906366-10-0 (paperback)

British Library Cataloguing-in-Publication Data

A catalogue record for this book is available from the British Library.

Printed in the United Kingdom

Capp Press uses environmentally responsible paper and does not use papers sourced from endangered old growth forests, forests of exceptional conservation value, or the Amazon Basin.

This is the fully revised and updated second edition of The Strengths Book, to match the updated strengths tool, Strengths Profile.

To our Capp clients, Capp family and friends for sharing with us your strengths in action every day.

Authors' preface

Alex's strengths journey

My strengths journey began in 1999 when I came across Martin Seligman's Presidential Address to the American Psychological Association, as he introduced 'positive psychology'. This essentially argued that since the Second World War, psychology had been overly focused on fixing what was wrong with people and hadn't done enough to build more of what was right with people.

Positive psychology was often described as being about 'happiness and human strengths'. There were a lot of people working in happiness, but less activity in strengths. I could also see a lot more real-world applications for strengths, so this was the path I chose – probably driven by my Strategic Awareness, Innovation and Legacy strengths (that I had yet to name).

I wrote some early thought pieces with Susan Harrington and conducted some important early research on strengths use with Reena Govindji (now Reena Jamnadas) – and subsequently discovered that I probably wrote so much because of my Writer, Explainer and Legacy strengths combined. As positive psychology took off in the popular imagination, I found myself increasingly in demand to deliver conference presentations and keynotes.

At one of these, I was asked a question that it turned out would determine at least the next decade and more of my life: "*What would it look like if somebody built an organisation based on strengths?*". The questioner was Nicky Page (now Nicky Garcea), who went on to become my co-founder at Capp. From what I remember, I did my best to answer the question, and seemed to conclude that it would be a really good thing to do and that somebody should do it.

It was around this time that I met Vernon Bryce, a quite brilliant business strategist and strengths practitioner, who said to me at the close of our very first meeting: "I can see you leading the Centre for Strengths Applications and Research" – a golden seed and master of Personalisation, if ever there was one. This validation from Vernon really got me thinking that maybe I could, in fact, do this.

The deal was sealed when I met with Nicky again, told her what I was planning to do, and asked if she wanted to join me. She said yes (key strengths – Optimism and Courage), and so Capp was born (in its original incarnation as the Centre for Applied Positive Psychology).

In getting started, we couldn't have done what we did without the faith and advocacy of early adopters including Karen Stefanyszyn at Norwich Union, Andrea Adams at BAE Systems, Dr Bob Hurling at Unilever, and Stephen Isherwood at Ernst & Young. They were brave enough to give our fledgling company a chance, and I am pleased to say that the results now clearly speak for themselves. The Capp team who have grown with us throughout this time stand as a testament to the power, pragmatism and purpose of a strengths-based organisation.

In working with Trudy on this second edition, we have also seen strengths come to life in many different ways through our diverse team and clients to leverage and maximise the talents of what different people do best (strengths of Creativity, Explainer, Improver and Writer).

As such, *The Strengths Profile Book* is not just a book, but a living testament to the power of strengths when applied in practice. Our goal in writing this second edition is to bring the power of strengths to life, so that you can fulfil your potential and realise your authentic best self.

Of course, writing any book is far from just a product of the authors whose names grace the front cover. There is always a team of unsung heroes behind the scenes who make it possible for those with Spotlight or Writer to step forward and take the author credits.

Professionally, huge thanks to our Capp colleagues and clients for being on the strengths journey with us. We learn from each and every one of you every day. Nicky Garcea especially, you are the embodiment of strengths-based working and complementary partnership. Thank you.

Personally, Jenny Linley is the Esteem Builder that anyone would need when taking on goals that are bigger than your current capabilities. Thank you. Jack, Lucy, Sophie and Ben have never known any different, so hopefully they are inspired with a belief in what is possible in their own lives. And Buddy and Dash, the family dachshunds, just give much valued perspective on everything.

Alex

Trudy's strengths journey

From my first Saturday job in retail through many years in occupational psychology, I've enjoyed success. I was ambitious, loved working with others to make things happen and always tried to exceed expectations, whatever task was set. I was lucky enough to be recognised for my efforts through changing roles and management of people. Like most, there were days that I enjoyed and days that I didn't, and I accepted this was how it should be. My mistake was never taking the time to understand what it was that made a good day good or a bad day bad. The outcome was a lot of successful days but a feeling of being drained.

Then I joined Capp. We were a small team then, but there was a lot of attention on listening, understanding and valuing people. Everyone was authentic, there was no judgement and I experienced my first 'appreciation circle'! Alex Linley and Nicky Garcea always looked for the best in me from day one. They regularly recognised me both publicly and privately for my achievements. They encouraged me to play to my strengths and challenged me to push myself further when they discovered my talents. They invested time to coach, mentor and develop me. They taught me how to channel my enthusiasm by building the business case for my ideas, and then trusted me to be responsible for the outcome. I loved what I was doing and felt valued for being me and what I did. When days were tough, I still enjoyed them. When things didn't quite go right, that feeling of failure had gone. Discovering strengths unlocked all of me, rather than relying on what others could only recognise in me.

Like most people, I've had challenges too. I used to gloss over the real issue, get my head down, hold my emotions in, and get through. After discovering my strengths (and weaknesses), I was able to reflect on why certain paths had attracted me and why some challenges were more difficult than expected. By using my strengths as a toolkit, I can now recognise what will be tough and when to ask for help.

Strengths development is a journey. It takes time and work. Whilst it might be common sense to work from your strengths, it isn't always common practice. Even if you think you know your strengths, you must still take them on a journey. Understand their history, use, benefits, and motivation. You can then go on to develop them, apply them, use the language, and of course celebrate them.

Strengths have changed my life and I hope I can give that gift back by helping you develop your strengths. My top strengths are Legacy and Mission, which makes me passionate about making a difference for future generations. I am privileged to enable coaches and organisations to understand and apply strengths, and I hope that through this book we can help so many more people find happiness and fulfilment with their strengths.

In summary, be happy, go for what excites you, pay attention to that feeling in your stomach, not just your head. It's never too early, or too late, to be your best self.

Special thanks go to Alex Linley and Nicky Garcea who saw something in me (the golden seed) and grew this. Also, my husband Gren and children, George and Grace, for demonstrating the miracles that can happen through love, laughter and belief in each other. I could not have written this book without my many clients who have shared their strengths stories with me – thank you.

Trudy

A special acknowledgement to the authors of the first edition

We give particular thanks to our colleagues who joined us for the first edition of *The Strengths Book*, but who have graciously passed on the baton for this second edition. Janet Willars, Robert Biswas-Diener, Nicky Garcea and Martin Stairs all played integral roles in the writing and production of *The Strengths Book* first edition, thereby laying the groundwork and foundations from which we have now built and continued for this second edition. Thank you.

Alex and Trudy

Contents

Part 1:

Introducing Strengths

Strengths Fact

The most common **realised strength** in the world is
Pride

To find out more about our global strengths data, visit
www.strengthsprofile.com

Introduction

Strengths Profile is a product developed by Capp.

Capp was founded in 2005 by Alex Linley and Nicky Garcea with a clear purpose of *Strengthening the World*, enabled through our vision of *Matching the world to their perfect job*. Our Capp staff are proud to contribute daily to the difference we make through strengths.

We've become *The Strengths Experts* through our hundreds of research papers and thousands of hours working on the application of strengths. Whilst we pride ourselves on our background in research and data, we've also listened and watched extensively for strengths in people in all areas of their lives. We are humbled to work in advising people and organisations across all professions and backgrounds to identify and develop their strengths. We know a strength from a mile off!

We started our journey in 2005 with 'Strengthspotting', a way of learning to identify, classify, and measure strengths through conversations. Through these conversations with individuals and organisations, we have over 200 validated strengths we work with to support our assessment, development and transformation interventions.

We work in the real world with people, managers, and organisations who want to know more about themselves from a holistic view. People who want to understand what they are good at, what they love to do, and what they have the potential to be good at in the future. There are also questions about things they are good at but didn't enjoy and yes, that question, *"What are my weaknesses then?"*.

To help with all of this, we developed an online strengths assessment, launched in 2009, that could identify and help people to develop their strengths, and could also address the other questions. We chose 60 of the most prevalent strengths from our bank of validated strengths and our thousands of interviews to develop what is now Strengths Profile (formerly Realise2 and R2 Strengths Profiler).

This book is all about the 60 strengths featured in Strengths Profile. Most of us don't have a clear understanding of what our strengths are, the things we **can do + love to do**. Through this book, and the Strengths Profile assessment, we'll show you how to develop these strengths so that you can become your best self.

If you have completed the assessment and already have your Strengths Profile, use the book to gain deeper knowledge of your own strengths and those of others too.

If you don't have a Strengths Profile, you can complete one at **www.strengthsprofile.com** or try these questions to get you thinking more about the strengths you have, in preparation for the next chapter.

- What do your friends and family know you for?
- Ask a friend to describe you at your best to a stranger – what do they say?
- When are you at your best inside of work?
- What do you enjoy most outside of work?
- What does a 'great' day look like for you?
- When did you last go home energised from work? Why was that?
- What tasks or activities do you find easy?
- What skills, through work or school, did you learn quickly?
- When did you last achieve something you were proud of?
- What made you feel this way?

What is a strength?

Research has shown that only one in three people can say what their strengths are. Unfortunately, of these people, most will still get it wrong.

When people talk about strengths, most people think about 'the things that I'm good at'. This is probably something ingrained from education. Hopefully, we will have been recognised and appreciated throughout our life for the tasks we do well.

And that's right, to an extent, but there is much more. Through the thousands of hours Strengthspotting, and reading all the research reports, books, conference abstracts and opinion pieces, we define a strength as consisting of:

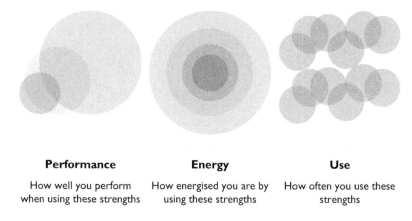

Performance	Energy	Use
How well you perform when using these strengths	How energised you are by using these strengths	How often you use these strengths

You can read more about this thinking in the book *Average to A+: Realising Strengths in Yourself and Others* by Alex Linley.

Performance

Performance is likely to be the one thing you have already recognised in yourself through your education and school. You might be good at, say, motivating the football team forward, writing essays, or coming up with new ways of doing things. For it to be a strength, you do need to be good at it. It's no good enjoying singing without any performance in it – unless you want to keep it as a hobby.

Energy

Let's look at the most critical element: energy. When you are using a strength, you feel energised. You get a buzz. You feel like it's the 'real you' coming through. You feel like you could use the strength all day. It's the activity that has you leaping out of bed in the morning earlier than usual. It's the work assignment that has you screeching to a halt, leaving tyre marks in the office car park, because you can't get to your desk fast enough. It's that sense of 'This is what I was born to do'. Strengths are deeply fulfilling to us – and they should be. They are about our unique selves, what we love to do and who we are at our best.

The science tells us that people perform better at work when using their strengths – and are a lot more engaged with what they are doing. People are happier when using their strengths, as well as feeling more capable and more confident in what they can achieve. Performance and energy contribute to this.

People grow, learn, and develop best in the areas of their strengths, despite the common mistake that our 'areas for development' should be our weaknesses. You can read more about the science of strengths on page 180.

In contrast, when you are good at something but don't have the energy in the task, we call this a learned behaviour. Whilst a valuable skill and resource, it is *not* a strength.

This is where people are often mistaken. They think that because they are good at doing something, it must be a strength. But for it to be a strength, you have to be good at it **and** energised by it. If you're just good at it but you don't enjoy it, then it's a learned behaviour. This realisation has been a lightbulb moment for thousands of people through our work.

Learned behaviours form part of our Strengths Profile Model of Development, which can be found on page 151.

Use

The third element of our strengths definition is use. If a strength isn't being used, we think this is something that needs some attention. If you perform well at something and enjoy it, but don't use it, you could be sitting on a potential talent to be utilised.

In Strengths Profile, we call these unrealised strengths.

In contrast, realised strengths are the things that you perform well at, find energising, and do frequently. We already use them to achieve good performance results.

Unrealised strengths may be new to us because we don't have the situation or opportunity to use them as much. This distinction between realised strengths and unrealised strengths is a powerful one. Quite simply, our areas of greatest potential for development exist in our unrealised strengths.

If you have a Strengths Profile, you will be familiar with your realised and unrealised strengths. If you are using this book on its own, as you go through the strengths and tick off the ones you have, pay attention to how often you use them currently. Give them a score out of 10 on use and mark any under 6 as an unrealised strength, with 7 and over being your realised strengths.

You can learn more about developing and applying your strengths in Part 3 of this book, starting on page 143.

Part 2:

The 60 Strengths

Strengths Fact

The most common **unrealised strength** in the world is

Mission

To find out more about our global strengths data, visit
www.strengthsprofile.com

Action

Understand me

I feel an overriding compulsion to act immediately and decisively. I'm much more comfortable with forward momentum than with careful strategy and reflection. As soon as I get an idea, I don't want to wait. Getting started is the only way for me. If it doesn't work out, then at least I had a try.

Describe me

"I always think 'Why wait?'. If I get a great idea or someone else comes to me with one, I want to act on it straight away."

"I seem to have a surplus of energy and often feel compelled to get going when asked to support on a task."

"If I don't know the answer to something I'm working on, I'm quick to enlist the help of others so I can get it done without delay."

"I don't like to sit on a task and think about it, getting started is the only way. That way I can see what works and learn quickly from any mistakes."

"I sometimes find the planning stage frustrating, or I'm quickly bored when working with others who work slowly."

People like me

Sir Bob Geldof – Irish singer rising to fame with the Boomtown Rats. He was awarded a knighthood in 1986 for organising Band Aid and other concerts that raised millions for African famine relief.

Daryl Hannah – American actress and environmental activist. She has been arrested many times for taking Action against environmental issues, including chaining herself to a tree.

Angelina Jolie – Oscar-winning actress and filmmaker. She is widely known for her successful humanitarian work supporting refugees, conservation and women's rights.

The Strengths Profile Book

Develop me

ⓒ Coach yourself

What energises you most about getting started and acting immediately?

In what situations does your desire to act reveal itself most strongly?

How do you deal with situations where you can't act quickly or where others may procrastinate?

✅ Apply yourself

Don't put off tomorrow what can be done today. Finish off any projects that have stalled. What one quick win will get you motivated and going again?

Who can you partner with who plans, but never seems to get going on a task? Note where others struggle and where you can successfully step in.

Take stock of everything that you or others achieve. Take the time to share your successes. Give credit where it is due to encourage yourself and others.

⚠ Watch out for yourself

Don't let your forward momentum cause you to crash. Your strength in acting quickly, decisively, and without hesitation can, if overplayed, result in you leading others down the wrong path. Leave sufficient space to pause, reflect and take stock.

Adaptable

Understand me

I love rearranging resources and adapting my plans to meet changing demands. I sense when to stay on track and when to deviate to become more effective. My adaptability means that I'm always looking for the best possible fit for things, being prepared to change as the context and need requires.

Describe me

"I love playing around with things to get the best possible result from reorganising and rearranging them."

"I enjoy being in the moment of having to rearrange the way a meeting or social event needs to run – perhaps if someone has overrun or cancels."

"I get such a buzz from someone coming to ask me 'How on earth will we get that done?' and having the answer."

"I can bounce between groups of friends or form collaborations with different colleagues easily as circumstances dictate."

"I prefer to have numerous friendships as I'm able to juggle many social responsibilities."

People like me

Heston Blumenthal OBE – Chef and restaurant owner. He is renowned as a culinary alchemist for the novel and innovative ways in which he combines foods.

Lady Gaga – American singer, songwriter, and actress. She is known for her unconventionality and provocative work as well as experimentation with new images.

Abraham Lincoln – Former US President who successfully led his country through the American Civil War. He signed the Emancipation Proclamation that ended slavery, changing American society for good.

Develop me

☺ Coach yourself

In what types of projects and situations do you most enjoy being flexible with your approach? Why is this?

What is it that energises you most about rearranging and adapting your plans?

What do you do that allows you to judge how things fit best and what can be adapted?

✓ Apply yourself

When changing and reacting to situations, explain your rationale to others so they can see your response is considered and not rushed.

Your ability to stay calm in the event of panic will reassure friends and colleagues. Support others to stay on track and see through any issues.

You enjoy variety, so seek roles that require a level head in a fast-paced environment. Try to avoid very structured tasks where approaches are constrained.

⚠ Watch out for yourself

Know when to leave well alone. Your strength in adapting plans could, if overplayed, be exhausting for others. Some people aren't as flexible and Adaptable as you. Be attuned to when a more stable and consistent approach will be more successful.

Adherence

Understand me

I have a natural focus on taking the right approach. I love following guidelines, rules, instructions and procedures. I feel most comfortable completing tasks that have clear steps and stages, where I'm trusted to follow these to the letter.

Describe me

"I work best when I know what I am supposed to do and when people know what to expect from me."

"I don't deviate from the rules. If the rulebook says it has to be done in such a way, then it must say it for a good reason."

"People usually feel safe and secure when relating and working with me. They know what to expect."

"If there isn't a process for something I am working on, nothing excites me more than to come up with one."

"I prefer tasks and roles where there is some strict structure in place, as I don't work so well without it."

People like me

Warren Buffett – American billionaire and philanthropist. He is Chairman of Berkshire Hathaway and recognised for having the same daily routine for decades.

Queen Elizabeth II – British monarch since her coronation in 1953. She is recognised for her Adherence to her coronation oath and the exemplary decorum of her public office.

Dame Jessica Ennis-Hill – British Olympic gold medallist. She is known for her strict diet and exercise regime throughout her athletic career.

Develop me

☜ Coach yourself

How does your ability to stick to the rules support you daily?

What do you do when there are limited guidelines or no guidelines to follow?

How do you work positively with others who don't enjoy operating within clear boundaries?

✓ Apply yourself

Don't let others persuade you that rules aren't important. You can bring structure and calm to chaos, which will benefit many.

Consider how to implement your rules positively. Explain the benefits it will bring and the rationale for the approach to ensure buy-in.

Get involved in something new at work or at home. Review the existing processes and make recommendations to develop a more efficient way.

⚠ Watch out for yourself

Don't stifle progress. Your strength in following guidelines, steps and stages to the letter can, if overplayed, hinder innovation. Allow space, when necessary, for the creative process to unfold – rules sometimes need to be tested and broken for new ones to emerge.

Adventure

Understand me

I relish the risk of the unusual or the untried. I look forward to experiences that are on the edge of, or outside, my comfort zone. New and challenging scenarios provide ways for me to test myself and to understand what I can and can't do. Above all, I love to push the boundaries and see what life will throw at me.

Describe me

"I love to travel to different places that people wouldn't normally associate with going on holiday."

"I find myself thinking about how I would react to new and difficult situations. It helps give me a deeper understanding of myself."

"I find it exciting to do something that scares me and that carries a real risk – something that takes me to the edge."

"I really enjoy experiencing new and challenging situations, and even more so if it is with others."

"I find that I am at ease with being uncomfortable to the point when I'm not. I look for ways to be challenged."

People like me

Bear Grylls – British adventurer, writer, and television presenter. He is widely known for his television series *Man vs. Wild*.

Prince Harry – British Prince. He and a group of military veterans reached the South Pole after a gruelling 200-mile-long (335 kilometres) trek in treacherous weather conditions across Antarctica for charity.

Valentina Tereshkova – Soviet cosmonaut. As the pilot of Vostok 6 in June 1963, she was the first woman to go into space.

Develop me

⊙ Coach yourself

What's the biggest risk you have taken? How did you benefit from it?

What gives you that buzz when you are at the edge of your comfort zone?

What impact does your sense of Adventure have on you or others around you?

✓ Apply yourself

Is there a task or project you would love to do right now but have put off? What one thing could you do to get closer to this?

Create a list of questions when considering a new approach, to weigh up the benefits of choosing a riskier or consistent approach. Share the results with others to gain trust.

Think through the impact of risk on others as you embark on another exciting Adventure. Consider ways to demonstrate your considered care and attention to their wellbeing.

⚠ Watch out for yourself

Don't become an adrenaline junkie. If overplayed, you could find yourself never settling with anything for any length of time. It could also impact negatively on your wellbeing and see you becoming bored in relationships. Learn to balance your need for Adventure with more routine activity.

Authenticity

Understand me

Whatever I do, I do it with genuine feeling and without pretence. I always keep to my own values and beliefs, no matter what people want me to do. Regardless of pressure from others, I'm proud to stand up for what I believe in, doing the things that are right for me, in the way that is right for me.

Describe me

"I am known for my integrity. People know that I will always follow the path that is right for me and aligned to my values."

"I can't think about behaving in any other way than being genuine."

"I prefer to be with friends and colleagues that accept me for who I am. It also means I expect others to be themselves in return."

"Sometimes I am the only one that feels different, but I still have to say something or I know I will burst."

"I find it really difficult to be in a situation that goes against the grain of who I am and what I believe in."

People like me

Maya Angelou – American author, poet, and political activist. She is known for her authentic quotes, and at the President's request read her now famous poem *On the Pulse of Morning* at the presidential inauguration ceremony in 1993.

Michael Moore – Documentary film maker and Academy Award winner. He has a reputation for politically liberal views and the ability to embrace public scrutiny.

Meg Whitman – Former CEO of Hewlett Packard and Ebay. She has a reputation for making tough and unpopular decisions that lead to company successes. She stays true to her desire to bring about change.

Develop me

☺ Coach yourself

Where does your strong sense of who you are come from? Has this changed over time?

Is there a situation when you held firm and maintained your Authenticity that makes you proud?

How does what you believe in guide your day-to-day actions and decisions?

✓ Apply yourself

Put yourself in situations where honesty may be challenging. A friend, a colleague, or a situation that cries out for a truthful approach is your speciality.

Encourage others to share their opinions when they feel challenged. Reassure them that it is okay for their beliefs to differ from others.

Take on roles and activities that align to your values. Remind others why the task is important, to keep everyone motivated towards a purposeful result.

⚠ Watch out for yourself

Know when to insist on being yourself, as well as learning when it's okay to flex a little. If overplayed, behaving in a way that is in keeping with what you believe in could jar with the situation. Judge your context and call on your Authenticity as required.

Bounceback

Understand me

Whatever the obstacle, setback, or disappointment I come up against, it just makes me more determined to succeed. Following disappointments, I love to pick myself up very quickly and use setbacks as a springboard to spur me on to prove to myself that I can achieve more than I would have done otherwise.

Describe me

"I've been through some real ups and downs in my life, but I've always managed to use them to come out on top."

"When a setback happens, I find myself saying 'I'll show you' and quickly turning the disappointment into a drive to do even better."

"It feels great to look back at a situation that didn't go as planned and think 'I've since done better for myself'."

"I'm confident to keep going during any conflict I experience in my relationships. After all, the best ones are worth fighting for."

"Someone once said that if you knock me down, I will come back stronger. I certainly look to learn from situations rather than dwell on them."

People like me

Jessica Cox – Motivational speaker. She was born without arms, and used her legs and willpower to become the first licensed armless pilot. She's also the first armless black belt in the America Taekwondo Association.

Andy Grove – Co-founder of Intel and the visionary behind their shift from memory to processor chips. Born in Hungary, he overcame tremendous hardship. His impact on the tech world is remarkable.

Wilma Rudolph – US Olympic gold medallist. First US woman to win three gold medals in track and field events, despite overcoming paralysis due to polio.

Develop me

☞ Coach yourself

Where does your ability to pick yourself up from a setback and do even better come from?

What enables you to maintain your determination to succeed? What resources do you draw on?

When has your ability to respond positively to setbacks been most helpful to you?

✓ Apply yourself

Get involved in a difficult task at home or at work where others have taken a back seat. Try working together to give them confidence as you listen to their advice.

Review your existing goals and priorities to push yourself further. Consider ways to reduce the time, increase the result, or spend less money.

Others may need more time than you after a setback. Use your inner motivation and drive to get them going again sooner.

⚠ Watch out for yourself

Don't become a struggle-seeker. If overplayed, your Bounceback can lead you to continually put yourself in, or be put in, situations requiring you to recover. Set aside time to learn from these experiences and rest, rather than moving straight from one to the next.

Catalyst

Understand me

I love to mobilise and inspire other people to take part in activities and projects. I particularly enjoy getting new projects off the ground and putting ideas into action by involving others. It's so rewarding getting people excited and motivated to work on things that otherwise they might never have done.

Describe me

"I find that new approaches are too exciting to pass me by. It's what I love to get involved in."

"If a project is going to make a big difference to the way we do things, I am quick to get people on board with my ideas."

"When someone I trust and respect gives me a great idea for a way forward, I find I am immediately getting others excited about it too."

"When I am working on a project with others, I'm the one who will continue to motivate people so that they embrace it as much as I do."

"I believe together we can achieve great things, but I do need encouragement to invest in relationships. I can get too excited about the next objective."

People like me

Mohandas (Mahatma) Gandhi – Political and spiritual leader. He pioneered satyagraha (civil disobedience) based upon ahimsa (non-violence) and led India to independence, inspiring movements for civil rights and freedom across the world.

Martin Luther King, Jr. – African-American clergyman, activist and civil rights leader. He inspired the civil rights movement through his famous *I Have a Dream* speech.

Danica Roem – American journalist and politician. In 2018 she became the first openly transgender person to be both elected and serve in any US state legislature.

Develop me

⟡ Coach yourself

What do you love about motivating and inspiring others?

What allows you to be so successful at getting others going on a project?

What situation or project have you initiated that you are most proud of?

✓ Apply Yourself

In what situations do you find the most inspiration? Consider even small changes and projects in the areas that bring the greatest reward to you.

Create a checklist when starting off a new project to ensure a considered approach. How will the change impact others? How will you measure success? Who will benefit?

When you have a great idea, try partnering with those who have strengths in Organiser and Planner to ensure you see your project through to the end.

⚠ Watch out for yourself

Don't lose your focus or spread yourself too thin. An overplayed strength in motivating others could result in abandoning your own responsibilities to others. Limit the number of projects you initiate. Commit time and effort to making these successful before moving on to the next.

Centred

Understand me

I feel as though I look out at the world with confidence. I'm grounded in the solid foundation of my sense of self and deep knowledge of who and what I am. I love to feel the natural sense of self-assurance that I maintain almost effortlessly in any situation.

Describe me

"I love that people ask me to do things all the time that perhaps they wouldn't do themselves."

"I'm known for my calmness in any situation. People have told me that they feel calm just listening to me speak and watching me approach something."

"I am asked to support difficult or new tasks because people know that I will not get into a panic."

"I feel at ease with myself in most situations. After all, you can only do your best and I often think 'What's the worst that can happen?'"

"I sometimes need a reminder when to show excitement as I can be too busy being calm."

People like me

HH Dalai Lama – The spiritual leader of the Tibetan people. He is a Nobel Peace Prize recipient in recognition of his leadership of the non-violent struggle for the liberation of Tibet.

Dame Vera Lynn – English singer. She became known as the Forces' sweetheart during the Second World War when her song *We'll Meet Again* became emblematic of the era.

C. B. "Sully" Sullenberger – US pilot. He landed a US Airways flight in the Hudson River following a collision with birds that destroyed both engines. He published the experience, *Highest Duty*, which features among the New York Times bestsellers.

Develop me

Coach yourself

Where does your inner confidence come from?

How does your strength in being Centred benefit you at work and at home?

When has your self-assurance been tested the most? What did you learn?

Apply yourself

People will hang on to your every calm word. Pay more attention to how and what you say in challenging situations, role modelling your approach to others.

Put yourself in situations where you take the lead in more complex or high-pressure environments. Help others to understand what you see.

Share your confidence and support others with difficult conversations. Your ability to remain calm will help to enable a more successful outcome.

Watch out for yourself

Don't forget to relax. You could convey a lack of enthusiasm or an unwillingness to move to action if overplayed. Know when to moderate your calmness and self-assurance with enthusiasm and spontaneity, recognising that sometimes it's better to reveal your feelings.

Change Agent

Understand me

I'm energised by change. I'm able to see the real benefits of change and always love to be involved with, and bring about, change in some way or another. I'm often an advocate for new developments and my enthusiasm for change enthuses others who may otherwise have been more reluctant.

Describe me

"I get excited by being in situations where I can pretty much do what I want and be able to explore new opportunities."

"I'm always keen to ensure I bring others on board with my ideas in a positive way. I want them to feel as excited as I do and buy in to the idea."

"I love being involved with a project that nobody else is doing. Even at home, I want to be the first to change the way we do something."

"It's not just the process of change that excites me, I love to identify the changes and consider all the benefits it will bring."

"I can get a little frustrated when the change process takes too long, as I love to get going immediately and see things through."

People like me

Mikhail Gorbachev – Former leader of the Soviet Union. He is best known for his dramatic policy reforms, including perestroika (restructuring) and glasnost (openness), along with his ability to work with non-communist heads of state.

Beverly Naidoo – South African children's author. She writes about her experiences under the apartheid regime and was arrested for her activities as part of the resistance movement.

Sheryl Sandberg – American technology executive, activist and author. She has encouraged a movement for women in her book *Lean In: Women, Work, and the Will to Lead.*

Develop me

⌣ Coach yourself

When were you first aware of being energised by change?

How does change benefit you and those around you?

How do you get others positively onboard when working with a change project?

✓ Apply yourself

Ensure your changes are well considered. Think about how it will impact those around you and what they will need to embrace the change.

Team up your strengths in motivation with those of Planner, Detail, or Organiser to ensure the project gets completed efficiently. Ask others for support if you don't have these strengths.

Support those who are more unsure about change. Highlight the benefits and values it will bring. Share your confidence in the end outcome.

⚠ Watch out for yourself

Avoid change for the sake of change. Your strength in involving yourself actively in the process of change can, if overplayed, lead to instability and uncertainty for other people. Learn when change is necessary, as well as when it isn't.

Compassion

Understand me

I have an open heart and care about all the people around me. I want the best for everyone, and offer sympathy and support to others, especially in times of suffering. When people are unhappy, I look for the right thing to say and aim to help people in whatever way I can.

Describe me

"I care deeply about the people I work with. I want to make sure they are happy and doing okay."

"People tend to come to me because they know that I care. It doesn't matter what the problem is, I just want to help."

"I feel it deeply when someone is suffering. When I can support them, I get a huge sense of satisfaction."

"Nothing gives me a greater feeling than knowing I have helped someone on the road to recovery. I like to make a difference."

"I have had to learn to recognise when people want my help. Not everyone wants sympathy and to be fussed over. This can be hard for me sometimes."

People like me

Sir Elton John CBE – British singer. He has sold more than 300 million records and his Elton John Aids Foundation has raised over $125 million.

Oskar Schindler – German industrialist. He is credited with saving 1,200 Jews during the Holocaust by employing them in his enamelware and munitions factories.

Mary Seacole – Jamaican-born British nurse. She applied to the War Office to serve in the Crimean War as a nurse, but was turned down. Unperturbed, she borrowed the money to make the 4,000 miles journey herself, treating the wounded from both sides while under fire.

Develop me

☺ Coach yourself

In what situations do you find yourself using your Compassion strength the most?

What impact does your Compassion have on you and on those around you?

How do you deal with others who are less compassionate than you are?

✓ Apply yourself

Take an active role during disagreements. Offer guidance – look beyond the conflict into how decisions will impact people's lives.

Help others at home or at work to make the difference you do in a subtler way. Suggest a fun charity event that they can all be involved in.

As well as showing you care deeply, move people on to an action they can embrace that will support their recovery and healing.

⚠ Watch out for yourself

Be careful not to suffocate people with your Compassion. If overplayed, your strength in reaching out to people when they are unhappy could be misguided. Know when Compassion may not be helpful and balance it with practical support and advice.

Competitive

Understand me

I just have to compete against others. Measuring my abilities relative to others is how I gauge progress and success. I love to make everything into a contest. I want to perform quicker and better than everyone at everything I do. For me, winning is the only option. Losing hurts.

Describe me

"I'm a very competitive person. I want to be the best at what I do."

"Whatever I am doing, I find myself starting to think about winning and how to beat the competition."

"Even if it is only small, I like to have something I can regularly call a win to make me feel as though I am competing."

"At work people are often surprised when we do something competitive; they see a side to me they don't often see."

"I tend to take it quite hard when I lose. I bounce back quickly but I don't go into situations not to win."

People like me

Muhammad Ali – Retired American boxer and three-time World Heavyweight Champion who would often provoke opponents or celebrate victories with his claim that "I am the greatest".

Billie Jean King – American tennis player. She is the winner of 12 Grand Slam women's singles titles, 16 Grand Slam women's doubles titles, and 11 Grand Slam mixed doubles titles.

Michael Phelps – Australian swimmer and Olympic medallist. He is the winner of a record 8 Olympic gold medals in the Beijing Olympics 2008 and holds the record for the most Olympics medals won by any athlete with 28, including 23 gold medals.

Develop me

✓ Coach yourself

When did you first notice your Competitive edge?

What does being Competitive achieve for you at home and at work?

When, or in what situations, are you at your Competitive best?

⚠ Apply yourself

Look for different ways to actively measure what you do. You may have missed opportunities at work to showcase your successes.

Introduce fun ways at home or at work to be more Competitive. Discover any hidden competitiveness with friends or colleagues with some friendly ways to win.

Don't just go from one win to the next without reflecting. Take time to understand why you won and to celebrate your achievements.

⚠ Watch out for yourself

Know when competition is unhealthy. If overplayed, your strength in measuring your success against others could impact negatively on your wellbeing and relationships. Know when competing will be detrimental to other things that are important in your life.

Connector

Understand me

Whatever situation I find myself in, I always love to make connections between the people that I meet. I notice when people have shared interests or something in common. I naturally make links between people and bring them together for their mutual benefit.

Describe me

"At parties I'm known for constantly introducing people to each other. I have a quick chat and move on quickly to see who else I can connect."

"I love bringing the right people together so that everyone has a good time and gets something from the meeting."

"I spend a lot of time thinking about who comes to the work or social events that I arrange. I like to ensure that there are people there who have something in common with each other."

"It's even more rewarding when you bring a diverse group together who don't appear to have much in common. I get such a buzz when they connect."

"As I'm such a social person, I could benefit from spending more quality time with people so I build deeper relationships."

People like me

Scott Gerber – Businessman and founder of the Young Entrepreneur Council, an organisation comprising the world's most promising young entrepreneurs and executives. He also co-authored *Superconnector*.

Katy Perry – US singer. She rose to fame with *I Kissed a Girl* and was the first person to exceed 100 million Twitter followers.

Klaus Schwab – German engineer, economist and founder of the World Economic Forum and the Schwab Foundation for Social Entrepreneurship. One of *Forbes* magazine's Top 100 Most Influential People in the World in 2009.

Develop me

⚙ Coach yourself

What motivates you to make connections between people?

What strategies do you use to build connections between people?

When has bringing people together made the biggest difference?

✓ Apply yourself

Consider your longer-term goals and any useful connections you could make now that would benefit you in the future. Lean in to others' networks too.

Use technology and social media, but ensure your interactions with others are meaningful. Connect with purpose and be clear on what you or others hope to gain.

As you make connections, grab a coffee or be sure to keep in touch. Take time to build relationships with those you reach out to.

⚠ Watch out for yourself

Don't forget to connect yourself. If overplayed, your strength in making connections between people could become a barrier to connecting with individuals yourself. If necessary, delay your capacity to connect others until you have got to know the person to whom you are talking.

Counterpoint

Understand me

I love to bring an alternative perspective to any situation. I seem to see things differently from others and can present a range of options, possibilities, and alternatives for any scenario. As a result, I often bring things into the discussion that other people have missed.

Describe me

"Whenever I am in a meeting, I find I need to sit on my hands until the time is right to share my idea. Not saying something is always a regret."

"I love to put forward different approaches to a discussion or situation. It can be on anything from wallpaper to parenting."

"The excitement for me is to bounce different ideas around and get people to think about things in different ways."

"I don't need to be an expert in a topic to have an idea about it. I use my instincts and experiences to guide what feels right."

"I can be known for a little arguing. However, I'm not offended if my ideas aren't taken forward. For me, the most important thing is to express my views."

People like me

Rachel Carson – American marine biologist and nature writer. Her book *Silent Spring* led to a reversal in US pesticide policy and popular interest in environmental concerns, prompting the establishment of the Environmental Protection Agency.

Nassim Nicholas Taleb – Author of *The Black Swan* in which he argues that one-off, unpredictable events can lead to massive consequences, contrasting with most other economic theories.

Dame Vivienne Westwood – British fashion designer. She is considered instrumental in bringing punk and new wave fashions into the mainstream and highlighting many causes. In 2014, she cut off her hair to highlight the dangers of climate change.

Develop me

☺ Coach yourself

What drives you to see things differently to other people?

What benefits does your Counterpoint bring to a discussion or situation?

How do others react to you sharing views and ideas on many topics?

✓ Apply yourself

Don't just come up with the ideas, formulate a plan and a business case. That way you will be far more credible and the idea is more likely to go ahead.

Seek out opportunities to be a guide, mentor, or adviser. Although you may not always know the answer, you have plenty of suggestions about possible approaches to offer.

Share your ideas in the appropriate way and at the appropriate time to ensure they are received positively. Try to get hold of any agendas for meetings in advance so you can be prepared.

⚠ Watch out for yourself

Know when not to be different. Your strength in always bringing things that others have missed into a discussion could come across as annoying and obstructive. Be prepared sometimes to join the majority consensus.

Courage

Understand me

While I may well feel afraid at times, my Courage means that I'm always able to face and overcome my fears. I get a buzz from participating in activities that make me nervous or scared. I never let my fear get in the way of what I want to do.

Describe me

"I like travelling, as I want to see and experience all there is to view and do in the world. It doesn't mean I always enjoy the unknowns that I may face on the way though."

"Overcoming my fears comes from within me. My heart volunteers for something before my head kicks in with the reality."

"I get as scared as others in challenging situations, but I push myself not to allow the fear to hold me back. The results are very satisfying, despite the sweat and tears."

"I don't take unnecessary risks, but I might find I say or do something that might be a bit unpopular as I'm not worried what people think."

"I'm drawn to the sense of achievement and this can mean I get myself in situations that I would, quite frankly, rather not be in!"

People like me

Sir Douglas Bader – Royal Air Force fighter ace. He fought in the Second World War despite having lost both his legs.

Harriet Tubman – First woman to lead an armed expedition in the American Civil War. She had previously helped slaves to escape using the network of activists and safe houses known as the Underground Railroad.

Ai Weiwei – Chinese contemporary artist and activist. He highlights human rights violations, has endured house arrest and been subjected to constant surveillance. He is an artist who puts his life on the line to defend freedom of expression.

Develop me

Coach yourself

How does your Courage help you to achieve your daily goals?

When have you felt the most scared but have gone ahead anyway? What did you achieve?

What enables you to face your fears when you are nervous?

Apply yourself

Mentor others by explaining your rationale for risk-taking. What makes you take that leap of faith? What are your strategies and resources?

Face your fears in areas that serve your goals rather than for the sake of the thrill. Make informed choices that serve a purpose and have benefits.

What still sits on your to-do list because of some element of fear? Set yourself a realistic goal around it and enlist the support of others to get going.

Watch out for yourself

Don't become a fear-facing addict. Your strength in doing what you want to do despite your fears can lead you to become addicted to seeking out fear-raising experiences. Create moments of calm – don't push yourself continually to face up to one fear after another.

Creativity

Understand me

Creativity is at my core. I love coming up with or combining new ideas, images, colours, tastes or concepts. I thrive on trying things that have not been tried before, linking things in novel and imaginative ways, and creating something.

Describe me

"I get quite excited when others get stuck for ideas on a project. I can't help getting involved by helping them to think differently."

"I am always thinking of ways that I can arrange things in a different way, and then I can't wait to get started on it."

"I enjoy making dull chores more interesting by being more imaginative about my approach to the task."

"Whether I'm preparing dinner or a presentation, I love to combine different things to come up with something new."

"I guess on occasions I should stick with what's already there as I can create work for myself – but then that wouldn't be me!"

People like me

Tracey Emin CBE – Controversial artist. She is one of the group known as the Young British Artists, a Turner Prize nominee, and Royal Academician of the Royal Academy of Arts in London.

Steve Jobs – Co-founder of Apple Inc. He created the iPod, iPhone, Mac, and other innovative brands that are renowned for their design and aesthetic appeal.

Beatrix Potter – Author and illustrator. She created 23 children's books featuring animal characters, the most famous of which is *The Tale of Peter Rabbit*.

Develop me

⏣ Coach yourself

How often are you able to use your Creativity? Would you like to use this strength more?

What's your incentive for doing things in a new and different way?

When has your Creativity made the biggest difference to you or others?

✓ Apply yourself

Try to ensure your work is varied with opportunities to do different tasks. You never know where you might be able to apply your ideas.

Recognise when your creative thoughts are at their best. Do you enjoying reading about a topic, talking to people, or simply just being quiet?

Ensure that while coming up with new ways of working, you research the best approach and the impact it will have so it is received positively.

⚠ Watch out for yourself

Don't just be a dreamer. Your strength in producing original work can, if overplayed, limit the extent to which you achieve anything concrete. Learn to balance your Creativity with a capacity to plan and to deliver, so that you bring your new and original ideas to fruition.

Curiosity

Understand me

I'm interested in everything. I'm totally open to new ideas and constantly seek out new information. I get excited when I discover new topics to study. I never let fascinating points pass me by without finding out more about them. I love to ask questions and do follow-up reading on things.

Describe me

"I love to ask questions to find out more. I find myself thinking of the next question before I've got the answer to the first."

"I'm always keen to learn more about situations. I don't take things at face value, I want to know more – exactly when and how."

"I enjoy talking to people about their experiences, however big or small. I love to get the intricate details, especially if it's something I don't know much about."

"I'm always reading various news stories and articles. You never know what you will learn or how you can apply your findings."

"I've learnt not to come across as nosey with all my questions, by making sure I interact with people in the conversation too."

People like me

Tycho Brahe – 16th century Danish astronomer. He carefully observed the night sky and a number of unusual astronomic phenomena such as a supernova.

Marie Curie – Twice Nobel Prize recipient. She was a physicist and chemist, noted for her discovery of elements and research on radiation.

Charles Darwin – Leading naturalist. He is credited with the discovery of the theory of evolution, which was published in *The Origin of the Species*.

Develop me

☺ Coach yourself

What benefits does your strength in seeking out new information bring?

What do you love about being curious and interested?

What was the last subject you researched? How did you apply this learning?

✓ Apply yourself

Focus your topics wisely to get the most from your learning. What are your own goals or challenges? What would be good to know more about?

Find activities where questioning is key. Try interviewing, coaching people, researching, or supporting a friend to get to the root of a problem.

Share your knowledge. Consider a variety of forums for your different audiences but don't hold on to your valuable learnings.

⚠ Watch out for yourself

Don't forget to act on your ideas. Your strength in always seeking out new information could impact negatively on your ability to get things done. It may also overwhelm people if you are constantly asking questions. Learn to spot when you need to move on from reflecting and into planning and action.

Detail

Understand me

I naturally focus on the smallest Detail and easily spot inconsistencies and mistakes. I get a great sense of satisfaction when I'm able to check that details are accurate and complete. Paying attention to Detail is very important to me – I would never submit anything myself that contained a mistake.

Describe me

"It doesn't matter what I'm doing, what I'm working on, or where I am, errors just seem to jump out at me."

"People often ask me to check their work as I get a real buzz from being able to correct errors."

"I always make sure that everything I do is properly finished off and that there are no mistakes."

"Every email that I send, I check through to make sure that the spelling and grammar are correct."

"I can be in a meeting or training and get distracted by a mistake in the presentation that no one else seems to notice."

People like me

Dame Zaha Hadid – British Iraqi architect. She was the consecutive winner of the Stirling Prize in 2010 and 2011 and is internationally known for her theoretically influential and ground-breaking architectural designs.

Sir James Murray – Scottish lexicographer and philologist. He was the primary editor of the *Oxford English Dictionary* from 1879 until his death.

Arlene Phillips CBE – English dancer and choreographer. She has worked on numerous West End and Broadway musicals and was a judge on BBC One's *Strictly Come Dancing*.

Develop me

☞ Coach yourself

Have you always loved to spot errors? When do you first remember doing this?

In what situation has your Detail been most valuable to you?

How do you balance your focus on Detail with your ability to deliver on time?

✓ Apply yourself

Be a role model rather than a critic. Create clear structured guidelines for people, at home and at work, to support others in creating error-free work.

Work with others who enjoy being creative. The powerful combination of great ideas being carefully implemented will shine through.

Don't get stuck with all the Detail. Note what types of work you enjoy proofreading and stick with this, rather than being a slave to other people's mistakes.

⚠ Watch out for yourself

Know when to settle for 'good enough'. Your strength in focusing on Detail can, if overplayed, hinder progress. Spot when a situation demands you to focus less on Detail, for example, when a piece of work needs to be delivered urgently. Dial your Detail strength up or down as the situation requires.

Drive

Understand me

I'm extremely self-motivated. I have an inner drive and motivation that pushes me to achieve more. I never need to be told what to do next. As soon as I complete one task I move on to the next. I love to set my own goals and targets, which are often higher than those that others may have set for me.

Describe me

"As soon as I have finished one task and ticked it off, I am already thinking 'What's next?'"

"I love to be busy. If I don't have much going on, it doesn't take long for me to find a task and get going again."

"I have a to-do list that I love looking at and rewriting. The best part is crossing things off it at the end of the day – no matter how small."

"I only feel like I have had a good day if I have achieved something. I don't like half-finished tasks."

"It can be difficult for me to relax at times and know when I have done enough for that day."

People like me

Alexander the Great – Macedonian king. He conquered 90% of the known world by the age of 32 years, campaigning as far as modern India and Pakistan before having to turn back because of a near-mutiny by his troops.

Amelia Earhart – American aviator. She was the first woman to fly solo across the Atlantic Ocean, for which she was awarded the Distinguished Flying Cross.

Malala Yousafzai – Pakistani activist. She is a human rights advocate, activist for female education, and the youngest Nobel Prize Laureate.

Develop me

☞ Coach yourself

Where does your inner motivation and Drive to succeed come from?

What enables you to continually maintain your Drive?

When has your determination to succeed been most helpful to you?

✓ Apply yourself

Understand how your other strengths play their part in your success. Don't just rely on your motivation, apply it with skill.

Slow down and consider what you want to achieve in the longer term. What can you work on today that will make way for this?

Understand and communicate the impact your tasks and approaches have on others before you begin. How will you all benefit?

⚠ Watch out for yourself

Know when to enjoy the moment. Your strength in pushing yourself hard to achieve what you want out of life can, if overplayed, impact negatively on your health and relationships. Strive for a balance that meets not just your desire to achieve things, but also your wider life needs and interests.

Emotional Awareness

Understand me

I'm an excellent judge of people's emotions and feelings. I want to know how people are feeling. I have a keen eye and intuitive ear. I can easily pick up on subtle clues and messages that people give out, making their emotions very clear to me.

Describe me

"I often notice if somebody is not happy, feeling slightly stressed, or just not themselves."

"I just seem to have this emotional barometer with people. They often talk to me about difficult and personal situations."

"It's easy for me to connect with others and I'm sensitive to minor emotional cues. I like to help them look for these."

"I find I can judge not only what to say, but how to say it to people, depending on their mood."

"I have learned that not everyone is as comfortable as me in identifying or talking about feelings."

People like me

Kiran Desai – Prize-winning novelist. She won the Man Booker prize for her novel *The Inheritance of Loss*, which focused on the emotional experiences of its protagonists.

Diana, Princess of Wales – First wife of Charles, Prince of Wales. She was known for her charitable work, particularly concerning AIDS awareness and landmines.

Robert Smith – Lead singer, guitarist, and songwriter. Through his music group The Cure, he is renowned for his ability to convey the full range of emotions through his music and lyrics, from deep, dark introspection through to quirky, upbeat pop.

Develop me

☞ Coach yourself

How do others respond to your Emotional Awareness?

What helps you become aware of what other people are feeling?

In what situations does being aware of the feelings of others benefit you most?

✓ Apply yourself

Don't shy away from situations involving conflict. You will be able to pick up on any unsaid comments and understand any emotional reaction.

Try working with larger audiences as you will easily be able to pick up on the emotions of the room and flex your approach or message.

Celebrate the successes of people that others may have missed due to their humble or subtle announcement.

⚠ Watch out for yourself

Don't be too sensitive. Your strength in picking up on subtle clues can, if overplayed, stifle your natural interaction with others. You may tend to comment on other people's emotions, which could leave them self-conscious or rob situations of their spontaneous nature. Know when to take people just as they are.

Empathic

Understand me

I have a natural connection with other people where I'm finely tuned in to them and can feel what they are feeling. I love to put myself in another person's shoes, to experience the emotions they are experiencing. I share their joy, their pain, their frustration and their elation.

Describe me

"I seem to feel just what other people are feeling. Happy or sad, I am there with you, laughing or crying."

"I'm always able to see things from another person's point of view. Doing this helps me to understand them or the situation better."

"I'm able to connect with others easily by expressing my genuine concern for them."

"I imagine what I would do in a situation, whether it's on the TV or real life. I often learn a lot about myself that way."

"It can be a little overwhelming at times, as I feel for everyone. I can't always turn it off."

People like me

Shah Rukh Khan – Indian Bollywood actor. He is the winner of 13 Filmfare Awards and renowned for his ability to connect with his audience.

Dame Esther Rantzen – Journalist and television presenter. She is well known for her work with charities and is the founder of the child protection charity ChildLine.

Carl Rogers – Influential American psychologist. He was one of the founders of humanistic psychology, developing the person-centred approach and client-centred therapy.

Develop me

Coach yourself

When did you first notice your ability to see things from others' points of view?

How do you build that special connection with people?

When is being Empathic most useful to you?

Apply yourself

Act as a sounding board to friends when they are helping or giving sensitive advice to others. Have they put themselves in the other person's shoes?

When offering support, always ensure you leave knowing what action the person is going to take. Follow this up to help them reach an outcome.

Consider different ways to be Empathic based on the person. It may not take grand gestures, but simply sitting with them could be enough.

Watch out for yourself

Protect your own emotional state. Your strength in tuning in to what other people are thinking can, if overplayed, lead you to become overwhelmed by other people's distress. Learn to protect your emotions by distancing yourself and remembering to attend to your own needs too.

Enabler

Understand me

I enjoy developing people to do things for themselves. At the same time as providing support and encouragement, I love to give people tasks and challenges that I know will stretch them, pushing them out of their comfort zone in ways that will help them to grow and develop.

Describe me

"I'm known for always saying to people 'You can do it'. I genuinely believe that with the right support they can."

"It gives me great satisfaction to see people become better and more confident at what they do."

"I really enjoy bringing out the best in people. I gradually give others more and more stretching jobs and then watch them grow and develop."

"If I'm not able to develop others, I'll still spot bursts of talent I see and tell the right people. It would be a shame to waste it."

"I occasionally need to make sure the people I encourage actually want my help, as sometimes people are happy where they are."

People like me

Brian Clough OBE – English football manager. He is the former manager of Nottingham Forest Football Club, who were twice consecutive winners of the European Cup in 1979 and 1980, despite having been promoted from the old Second Division only two years before.

Maria Montessori – Italian educator. She was the founder of the Montessori system of schools, which places the capabilities and interests of the child as central, treating them as competent beings capable of making their own decisions.

Tony Robbins – American self-improvement guru and best-selling author who has helped millions to improve their lives and is best known for his book *Awaken the Giant Within*.

Develop me

⚙ Coach yourself

How do others react to the stretching challenges you set them?

What do you wish to achieve by giving people new challenges?

What's been your proudest memory when you have enabled someone?

✓ Apply yourself

Take new people under your wing. Whether it's at work or in your hobbies, help them to hit the ground running by showing them the ropes, who's who, and how to get ahead.

Be specific in your positive feedback to support growth. What did you see? How did it benefit others? What strengths were they using? What was the impact?

Get involved in delegating tasks to others. Who could learn from your home skills (cooking, sport, DIY) as well as your work skills (mentoring, shadowing, software)?

⚠ Watch out for yourself

Don't push too far or too fast. Your strength in creating the conditions for people to grow and develop can, if overplayed, be misdirected. Spot when you are pushing someone too far out of their comfort zone and let people find their own level and pace.

Equality

Understand me

Being fair and equitable is at the heart of who I am. I consider everyone to be my equal and give great attention to issues of fairness and Equality. I love to make sure that all people are treated equally and that my own actions and decisions are as fair as they possibly can be.

Describe me

"I absolutely believe that everyone should be treated fairly and equally, no matter what."

"Whatever I am doing, I strive to get a fair outcome for all. I love to create win-win situations where everyone is treated equally and with respect."

"I'm uncomfortable in situations whereby winning creates a loser, as it can result in negativity and hurt feelings."

"I hold in high esteem those leaders who demonstrate and role model equality and fairness in all that they do."

"I try to remember that my views are my own perspective on how things should be, as I don't want to leave people feeling uncomfortable."

People like me

Emmeline Pankhurst – British suffragist. She was the founder of the Women's Social and Political Union, who campaigned for women to be given the right to vote.

Eleanor Roosevelt – US First Lady. She was chair of the Presidential Commission on the Status of Women from 1961-62 and is credited with helping launch the second wave of feminism.

William Wilberforce – British politician and philanthropist. He was a leading activist for the abolition of slavery, heading the parliamentary campaign that led to the passage of the Slave Trade Act in 1807.

Develop me

☼ Coach yourself

What is it that drives you to make sure that people are treated equally?

What impact does your focus on fairness and Equality have on others?

How do you respond to others who are less focused on fairness than you are?

✓ Apply yourself

You will be great at resolving conflict. You can ensure everyone is listened to and you will do your best to obtain a fair outcome.

Consider ways you can get involved in resourcing and task allocation or facilitating and chairing groups. You can help alleviate any friction and allow for everyone's involvement.

Partner with someone or use your own Mission, Legacy or Strategic Awareness strengths. Channel your energy on a relevant longer-term outcome with the goal of fairness.

⚠ Watch out for yourself

Don't be equal for the sake of it. Your strength in paying great attention to issues of fairness can, if overplayed, hinder what is best for individuals or the situation. Focus on what is right for individuals and the results being achieved – as well as for their enjoyment, wellbeing and development.

Esteem Builder

Understand me

My words and actions help to build self-confidence and self-esteem in others. I see potential and possibility in people and help them to recognise it for themselves. Through my relationships, I give people an understanding of what they are good at, even when they do not recognise it themselves.

Describe me

"I love to help people recognise what they are capable of, particularly people who might find it hard to accept positive feedback."

"I naturally look for ways to build people's confidence and self-esteem. It's so rewarding when they get to achieve something they never thought they would."

"I'm always coming across people who don't believe in themselves. I look for subtle ways to share what I've seen them do."

"I naturally correct people's language so it turns into more of a 'can do' and 'I can' attitude – even people I don't know."

"I'm conscious of personalising my praise, as I'm aware that not everyone likes a public display of recognition."

People like me

Jane Addams – Regarded as one of the founders of modern social work through her work in the US Settlement House movement. She was the first American woman to be awarded the Nobel Peace Prize for her international peace efforts.

Baloo the Bear – Fictional bear in Rudyard Kipling's *The Jungle Book*. He is mentor to the boy Mowgli and helps the boy to believe that he can achieve what he wants to achieve.

Yves Saint Laurent – French fashion designer. At age 21 he was the head designer of the House of Dior and is regarded as one of the foremost fashion designers in the 20th century.

Develop me

☺ Coach yourself

What is it that energises you about helping people see what they are capable of?

How, specifically, do you build people's understanding of what they can do?

What's your proudest moment of using your Esteem Builder?

✓ Apply yourself

Look for opportunities that put you in a position to develop, mentor, teach or facilitate. Your natural ability to boost confidence will be very rewarding.

Adapt your style according to your audience. You may need to be subtler in some contexts to ensure you sound sincere.

When giving feedback, try Strengthspotting (see page 144). What led the person to be successful in that situation? Be specific about what you observed so that it sticks.

⚠ Watch out for yourself

Don't over-flatter. Your strength in seeing the possibilities in other people and helping them to see what they are capable of can, if overplayed, be interpreted as being inauthentic. Be careful to maintain your authenticity as you help others to develop their self-belief.

Explainer

Understand me

I love to simplify things so that people can easily understand. I can take a complex idea and express it simply and clearly, so it is accessible to a wide range of people. If someone doesn't understand my explanation the first time, I enjoy coming up with different ways of explaining it.

Describe me

"I love being able to take some of the more technical areas I'm involved in and present them in such a way that people understand."

"I break things down using simple language that everyone understands. It doesn't need to be rocket science."

"I observe people I talk to, seeing how they respond, and asking lots of questions, just to make sure that they have got it."

"I have a natural tendency to teach others. I enjoy sharing topics and interests with others through my explanations."

"I have taught myself that not everyone shares my passions, so I look for clues of their interest before launching into teacher mode."

People like me

Brian Cox OBE – English physicist. He is best known as the presenter of various BBC science programmes and popular science books, making complex science accessible to and understood by all.

Malcolm Gladwell – Staff writer. He has worked for *The New Yorker* magazine and is the author of *The Tipping Point*. He is renowned for his ability to explain scientific and social concepts to a lay audience.

Delia Smith CBE – Best-selling UK cookery author. She taught thousands of people to cook for themselves through her television series and cookery books.

Develop me

☞ Coach yourself

In what situations are you most effective at explaining concepts and information?

How do you use your Explainer strength on a daily basis?

What impact does your ability to simplify things have on others?

✓ Apply yourself

Challenge yourself by varying your audiences. Try more senior, more diverse, or larger groups. What did you learn?

Be tuned in to your audience. Note when they look engaged, tired, bored or confused, and act accordingly. Know when to take a break.

Try new ways to explain yourself through quizzes, videos, images and demonstrations. Ask for feedback on what your audience liked best and anything that didn't work so well.

⚠ Watch out for yourself

Don't patronise. Your strength in simplifying things so that people can understand them could result in you explaining everything, to everyone, all the time. Try letting people work things out for themselves, as this can be a valuable part of the learning process as well.

Feedback

Understand me

I enjoy giving people both positive and negative Feedback. I believe that it is important for people to know what they have done well, so that they can build on it and progress. Equally, I let people know where they can improve, delivering my Feedback accurately, fairly and constructively.

Describe me

"People appreciate the fact that I'm always open and honest with them – it's the only way to be."

"I feel compelled to 'have a word' with people so they know whether they are on the right track, or if they should try something different."

"When I'm giving someone constructive feedback, I try to impart any knowledge I have to help them with the learning."

"I enjoy evaluating and commenting on other people's actions and decisions, so that they can see the impact they have, or could have, in the future."

"I always ask permission before launching into feedback, as I know not everyone always welcomes what I might have to say."

People like me

Marva Collins – American educator. She is renowned for working with disadvantaged students, using the Socratic method of classical education to help them succeed and flourish.

Simon Cowell – Television personality and music producer. He is renowned for his direct Feedback on *The X Factor, Britain's Got Talent* and *American Idol. Time* magazine twice named him amongst the Top 100 Most Influential People in the World.

Sir Alex Ferguson – Football manager. He managed Manchester United Football Club for 27 years and is said to be one of the greatest managers of all time. He is nicknamed 'the hairdryer' for the Feedback he gives his players.

Develop me

⊙ Coach yourself

When has your use of Feedback really made a difference?

What enables you to be successful at giving Feedback?

How do you yourself respond to Feedback?

✓ Apply yourself

Consider the Feedback you give. Don't sandwich constructive Feedback in between positive Feedback – the positive will be forgotten. Stick to the point.

Lead the way for Feedback at home and at work. Encourage a culture where at the end of the day, or in a meeting, you pause and ask how the person found it and what would make it better next time.

Don't forget to invite Feedback on your own work, as well as feeding back on others. Consider the Feedback you would give yourself too and act on any improvements.

⚠ Watch out for yourself

There's a time and a place. Your strength in providing fair Feedback to others can, if overplayed, lead you to provide it at inappropriate times or contexts. Know when to stop yourself from giving Feedback as it's not always welcome – however much you think people might need it.

Gratitude

Understand me

I'm constantly aware of how fortunate I am. I have a natural inclination to notice and appreciate the good things that happen to me. I don't take anything or anyone for granted. Each day I feel privileged to be who I am, being grateful for the life I lead and the positive things within it.

Describe me

"If something is going really well, however small, I tend to have a little sigh of contentment to myself."

"I love it when everyone is happy working or getting on well. I tend to point out subtle things like this to others to give them a little lift during the day."

"I like to thank, praise and compliment – often when people least expect it."

"I enjoy taking timeout moments during the day, just to be thankful when things go well. I love to capture those moments."

"I'm often telling people it doesn't take much to say thank you. Even if I don't say it, I get frustrated when I see people take something for granted."

People like me

Halle Berry – Actress. She won the Best Actress Academy Award for her role in *Monster's Ball* and is renowned for her acceptance speech in which she expressed extensive Gratitude to a long list of people who had supported her.

Robert Emmons – American psychologist. He is a leading Gratitude researcher, having developed the GQ-6 Gratitude Questionnaire and is the founding editor-in-chief of *The Journal of Positive Psychology*.

David Steindl-Rast – Austrian-American theologian. He is recognised for his active participation in interfaith dialogue and is a renowned writer on the topic of Gratitude.

Develop me

Coach yourself

What has taught you to be so appreciative for the good things in life?

How do you use your Gratitude strength during your day?

What benefits does your strength in Gratitude bring to you and to others?

Apply yourself

You can see perspective in challenging situations. Be that calming influence who can focus the team on where you have come from and what you can achieve.

Help others to feel appreciated by taking time to value and celebrate people's contributions to tasks and projects. Be as specific as you can about the impact they had.

Teach others a growth mindset by supporting them to appreciate what they learned during more difficult times, as well as how they can apply the learning next time.

Watch out for yourself

Don't give thanks without being authentic. Your strength in being thankful for the good things in life can, if overplayed, cause you to give thanks for everything. It could be perceived as being insincere, so learn to moderate when, and how often, you show your appreciation so that it always has the positive impact you intend.

Growth

Understand me

I actively seek out activities that will help me to develop, whether they are new skills, new knowledge, or a different way of doing things. I love to invite feedback on my performance, taking on board both positive and negative comments that will help me improve my performance and develop as a person.

Describe me

"I feel as though I am successful when I am learning a new topic. I try to learn something new every day."

"Even within subjects I know about, I delve deeper to find new angles, concepts, research and ideas to add to my learning."

"I'm always looking to see if there are different ways that I can develop and improve my skills, no matter what I am doing."

"I love the whole experience of learning. The process of acquiring new skills and knowledge and getting feedback is brilliant."

"I've learnt to allow others to go at their own pace. I'm conscious to gently share the benefits of growth rather than push them."

People like me

Florence Bascom – Geologist and academic. She was only the second woman to be awarded a PhD in Geology, going on to become the first woman to be part of the Geological Survey of America in 1896, and later became the first woman to hold any office as its Vice President.

Mihaly Csikszentmihalyi – Hungarian-born polymath. He is the author of numerous books, including *Flow: The Psychology of Optimal Experience.*

Socrates – Greek philosopher. He recognised that "The wise man is the man who knows how much he does not know".

Develop me

☞ Coach yourself

What is your ultimate goal? What are you striving for?

What do you love about developing new skills and knowledge?

How does your Growth strength help you achieve your goals?

✓ Apply yourself

Vary your learning style and acquire new skills in different ways. Try on-the-job learning, videos, reading, sharing with others, online and classroom learning. Note your preferences.

Bring others with you when you learn. Get them interested in your knowledge areas, share your top tips and enable their skills for better performance.

Push yourself outside of your comfort zone. What new areas can you look to grow in, that you may have shied away from to date? Which strengths will help you?

⚠ Watch out for yourself

Don't be too self-indulgent. Your strength in focusing actively on your personal growth and development can, if overplayed, result in you becoming self-absorbed. Find a balance that considers others' needs and interests, particularly those people who are closest to you.

Humility

Understand me

I'm a humble person, never allowing myself to be big-headed or boastful. Although I feel satisfaction with a job well done, I tend to give other people credit for my successes rather than take the credit myself. I know how much I depend on others for achieving things, and I appreciate and value their support.

Describe me

"I feel very honoured to be part of a successful team. I've had the pleasure to work with some really bright and talented people."

"When working with others, I know that our achievements are down to everyone's hard work and commitment, and that my role is often just a small part."

"When people congratulate me, I feel a bit uncomfortable. I'm quick to point out that it is because of others' hard work that the project was such a success."

"I know within myself that what I contribute is valuable, but I don't think that I am better than anyone else."

"I sometimes need to be careful that I don't overlook the contributions I make, as I don't shout about my successes."

People like me

Catherine, Duchess of Cambridge – As well as her charitable work, she can be spotted shopping in supermarkets and wearing high street clothes despite her royal status.

Keanu Reeves – American actor. He gave away almost 85% of his earnings from *The Matrix* to the special effects and costume design team; "Money is the last thing I think about", he said.

Darwin Smith – Businessman and former Chairman and Chief Executive of Kimberly-Clark who built the company into a consumer products giant. He had little interest in joining high-profile groups and associations.

The Strengths Profile Book

Develop me

☿ Coach yourself

What benefits does your strength in Humility bring to you and others?

What drives you to give credit to others, rather than to take the credit for things yourself?

How does your Humility manifest itself on a daily basis?

✐ Apply yourself

When pointing out the contributions of others, be factual and authentic. Recognise the individual and team strengths used, the diversity of the team, and the difference the outcome has made.

Work with those who seem to lack confidence. Let them know how they contribute to the team or group, and the positive impact this has.

Don't forget to include yourself when celebrating others. Ensure you raise awareness of the achievements you make, as well as the projects you were collaboratively involved in.

⚠ Watch out for yourself

Don't hide your light. Your strength in valuing other people for successes can mean that you avoid credit for your own achievements. This could result in others not appreciating your contribution or potential. Balance Humility with the confidence to talk about what you have achieved yourself.

Humour

Understand me

I love making people laugh and look for every opportunity to do it. I'm able to see the funny side of things and like to share this with others. I can crack a joke, or tell a story that lightens the mood, gives enjoyment to others and helps people relax.

Describe me

"I overcome my fears by making light of them, turning them into something funny for everyone to laugh at."

"I'm able to put people at ease with my humour. I have a talent for easing tense situations."

"Whatever I'm doing, and whoever I'm doing it with, I'm always trying to cheer people up."

"I can make any situation seem funny – I just love making people laugh."

"I have had to learn that some situations are simply serious and don't require me to be funny."

People like me

Ronnie Barker OBE and Ronnie Corbett CBE – Universally known as The Two Ronnies, icons of British comedy and creators of the iconic 'Four Candles' sketch.

Kevin Hart – American actor and stand-up. He won Billboard's Top Comedy Tour in 2016, using Humour as a way to cope with his troubled early family life.

Amy Schumer – American comedian and actress. She uses her Humour to raise awareness of social issues and in 2015, was named one of *Time* magazine's Top 100 Most Influential People in the World.

Develop me

ⓒ Coach yourself

What do you love most about making people laugh?

What do you achieve through your use of Humour?

When necessary, how do you dial down your Humour?

✓ Apply yourself

Take advantage of your skill to naturally engage with audiences. Be confident in presenting and making your explanations more memorable.

Focus your Humour, don't use it just for the sake of it. Who could do with cheering up or seeing the lighter side of a situation? Meet them for coffee and take their mind off any issues.

Humour has a positive effect on others. Use it to form social bonds and develop authentic relationships.

⚠ Watch out for yourself

Know when Humour is not funny. Your strength in making people laugh and lightening the mood can, if overplayed, cause others to never take you seriously. Learn to spot when Humour is not welcome. Rein in your desire to always deliver the punchline at these times.

Improver

Understand me

I get a thrill from seeing how I can make things more effective. I love looking for ways to do things better, even when I'm not asked to! I have an innate sense of how to improve on any way of doing things.

Describe me

"I believe that anything can be done better, you just need to review something with fresh eyes and have done your research."

"I have a reputation for being good with processes. Technology is constantly changing, so there are always new ways to approach a task."

"I love to take something that isn't working as well as it could and make it simpler, clearer, more logical, more efficient or simply better."

"I never have to be told when to improve something – even if it isn't something I am working on. I just naturally do it."

"It's been hard to learn that sometimes things don't need improving and that the way they are is good enough."

People like me

Mary Anderson – Inventor of the windscreen wiper. She was awarded a US patent in 1903, thereby improving the driving experience and safety of millions.

Elizabeth Fry – English humanitarian. She was known for her activism for prison reform. From 2001 to 2016 she was depicted on the Bank of England £5 note.

Jack Welch – Former CEO of GE plc. He was renowned for always striving for greater efficiency and higher profits, with his time at GE increasing the company's value by 4000%.

Develop me

Coach yourself

What drives you to look for better ways of doing things?

When have you used your Improver strength to achieve an outcome that you are proud of?

How do you judge when it's suitable to leave things as they are?

Apply yourself

Surround yourself with a role or hobby that allows you to learn, grow, and develop new and improved ways of working. You may feel stifled if you don't.

Measure the success of your improvements before moving on to the next thing. Use this as the business case for your next idea.

Be the gatekeeper of ideas on a new project to ensure that you make considered recommendations. Collate all the suggestions and record both the short and long-term benefits.

Watch out for yourself

Know when to leave well alone. Your strength in suggesting and making improvements can, if overplayed, mean you never rest or accept that things are satisfactory. Learn to spot when something does not need refining or improving, but can safely be left as-is – and then relax!

Incubator

Understand me

I love to think, to ponder, to reflect. I like to take moments out of my day, week, or month to give myself dedicated thinking time, to think deeply about things. These times are very precious to me, allowing me the time and space to be absorbed in my own thoughts without annoying distractions.

Describe me

"I work best when I have the chance to mull something over, rather than make instant decisions."

"When I talk to people I need to give myself time to reflect on what and how something was said, and then bounce it around for a bit."

"Decision-making takes me longer than others as I must think things through, but I'm then able to come up with the right way forward."

"I enjoy giving myself time to hold something in my head for a while and not consciously work on it, as the answer often then just pops out."

"If I am working things through, I've learned to let people know this so they don't think I'm just disinterested or ignoring them."

People like me

Dorothy Hodgkin – British chemist. She won a Nobel Prize for Chemistry after she deciphered the structure of insulin following 35 years of work.

Isambard Kingdom Brunel – British engineer. He was best known for his creation of the Great Western Railway. He reputedly would sleep on difficult engineering problems.

Jose Saramago – Portuguese writer. He did not write his first novel until he was in his mid-50s and was awarded the Nobel Prize in Literature when he was 76.

Develop me

Coach yourself

How do you ensure you make time to think things through when you are busy?

What drives you to give a lot of thought to things or important decisions?

What impact does your love of reflecting have on others?

Apply yourself

Get organised where possible, so you can do your thinking in advance. Read up on the subject or ask for an agenda before a meeting.

Limit distractions for set periods of the day to focus on thinking time and try blocking out time in your diary. It's essential, not a luxury.

Try partnering with those who like to make quicker decisions when a deadline is imminent. Bounce ideas around to stimulate your thinking and provide you with reassurance.

Watch out for yourself

Don't ponder on everything. Your strength in taking time to reflect can, if overplayed, see you come across as self-absorbed and unresponsive. Not everyone will want time to reflect. Learn to spot when a quicker or more decisive approach is necessary.

Innovation

Understand me

I want to be the first to design and create things that are new and have never been thought of. I can look at things from a different perspective to others, thinking laterally and 'out of the box'. My ideas and inventions help move things forward.

Describe me

"I don't get blinkered by what exists now, but look beyond this and into the realms of what could be."

"Nothing gets me more excited than someone saying, 'I don't think that can be done'. I'm often finding out more before they've finished the sentence."

"I am always trying out things from scratch, coming up with ideas that have never been tried before, and seeing what I can do to get them to work."

"I've usually got a few ideas bubbling around in my head that haven't come to fruition yet. I just enjoy having them there."

"I've learned to pause before going off with my ideas to make sure the tried and tested way isn't in fact a better one."

People like me

Sir James Dyson – British inventor, industrial designer, and founder of the Dyson company. He took thousands of failures to get his product right. As a result, he is best known as the inventor of the Dual Cyclone bagless vacuum cleaner.

Jacqueline Gold CBE – CEO of Ann Summers. She was the originator of the concept of women-only home parties. In 2016, she was awarded a CBE for her services to women in business, entrepreneurship and social enterprise.

Leonardo da Vinci – Italian artist, anatomist and inventor. He is widely credited as being one of the most innovative people in the history of the world.

Develop me

☺ Coach yourself

What's your earliest memory of being innovative?

What drives you to come up with new ways of doing things?

When have you achieved a particularly successful outcome using your Innovation strength?

✓ Apply yourself

Understand when you get your best ideas so that you can encourage this. Are you sat doing nothing, on a walk, exercising or watching TV?

Spend time with other creative people to bounce your ideas around, and with people strong in organising to help your ideas come to fruition.

When you need buy-in for your ideas, communicate clearly the benefits, rationale and way forward.

⚠ Watch out for yourself

Don't innovate for the sake of it. Your strength in being able to come up with new ways of doing things can, if overplayed, be obstructive rather than constructive. There's a time and a place for lateral thinking. Learn to spot when your desire for Innovation is going to be a hindrance rather than a help.

Judgement

Understand me

I make decisions quickly and easily. I enjoy quickly assessing the evidence of any situation. I'm confident that I will reach the right decision through my rapid analysis and weighing of the facts. I take pride in the fact that my decisions stand up to robust challenge, and usually turn out to be right.

Describe me

"Making decisions just seems to come naturally to me. As well as weighing up the facts, I apply my experience and perspective too."

"To others it might look like I sometimes rush decisions, but I have all the important points uppermost in my mind."

"People come to me all the time asking for my advice, often in subjects I'm really not very experienced in."

"I like to look at a situation and list the pros and cons in my head before deciding. It doesn't take long."

"I'm so confident in my own decisions that I must remind myself to run them past others and seek their advice on occasions."

People like me

Sandra Day O'Connor – First female member of the United States Supreme Court. She founded the O'Connor Institute, which ensures important policy decisions are made through a process of civil discussion and critical analysis of facts.

King Solomon – Described in the Bible as the King of Israel. He was revered for his wisdom and the legend of the Judgement of Solomon, in which he adjudicated who was the true mother of a disputed baby.

Sam Walton – Founder of retailer Walmart. He held Saturday morning meetings for all employees and their families, which supported a transformation of decision-making.

Develop me

ⓒ Coach yourself

What enables and guides you to make the right decision quickly and easily?

How do others value your decision-making ability?

In what situations does your strength in Judgement work best?

✓ Apply yourself

While the reasoning and benefits may be clear to you, take time to explain them to others in order to evidence your decisions and get people's support.

Speak up. Your clear judgements can be very persuasive with others. Confidently express the views of your team or family on important topics.

Put together a checklist of things to consider when making decisions. Consider milestones, stakeholders, processes, challenges and benefits.

⚠ Watch out for yourself

Consider the wider perspectives. Your strength in making the right decisions can, if overplayed, leave you closed to wider opinions or perspectives. Make time to seek and incorporate the views and opinions of others. Use this to refine your own decision-making processes.

Legacy

Understand me

I care deeply about future generations and seek to leave a Legacy through what I do. I enjoy working on things that make a difference and will have a positive impact on others. In whatever I do, I want to ensure that I create something that will outlast me and continues to make a positive contribution after I've gone.

Describe me

"It is my goal that one day my work will live on without me. What I leave behind is important to me."

"I firmly believe that we should all leave the world a better place than when we entered it."

"In everything I do, I think about the impact it will have on the people who follow me. They, in turn, can improve on this and impact future generations."

"There is so much we can do to make a difference. I love to learn from people who have left behind their ideas in books and quotes."

"The future excites me, but I have learned that without putting in the effort today, there won't be a future worth having."

People like me

Vint Cerf – American computer scientist. He is credited with developing the TCP/IP technology that enables internet communication and is referred to as the 'Father of the Internet'.

Wangari Muta Maathai – Founder of the Kenyan Green Belt Movement. She was an environmentalist focused on planting trees, environmental conservation and women's rights. She has a road named after her in Nairobi.

Baron Young of Dartington – Founder of the Open University. He created the learning facility that has gone on to educate millions of people who may not otherwise have had access to education.

Develop me

⚙ Coach yourself

In what ways do you want to leave a lasting positive impact on future generations?

How does your Legacy strength affect your daily decisions at work and at home?

How do you currently satisfy your Legacy strength?

✓ Apply yourself

Consider roles or tasks where you decide on and oversee the outcomes, ensuring your team or family all share your vision.

Explain your passions and inspirations so others know why your causes are important. Share your knowledge, thoughts and ideas so that other people can get involved.

What difference could you make in your local community? Is there something you could start, take over or stop that would have a positive impact?

⚠ Watch out for yourself

Don't become a slave to the future. Your strength in caring deeply about future generations can, if overplayed, limit the extent to which you live in the present. Balance your focus on your cause, with an ability to relax and 'enjoy the moment' from time to time.

Listener

Understand me

I show a keen interest in what people have to say and the way that they say it. When people are speaking to me, I focus intently on them and what they are saying. I listen not only to the words, but to how those words are used. Everything that someone says is important – I don't miss a thing.

Describe me

"Listening closely to someone is a big compliment to them. Everyone loves to be listened to and I love to do that for people."

"I find everyone interesting. I enjoy listening to people's stories as they are all fascinating to me."

"When I listen to people, I focus completely on the person talking so that they know I am listening. I shut out the entire world."

"My friends love coming over for a drink and telling me about their problems. I'm always there for them and I enjoy it."

"I sometimes need to remind myself to talk as well as listen, so that people know I'm still in the conversation."

People like me

Stephen Covey – American author. He was an advocate of listening through "Seek first to understand, then to be understood", found in *The Seven Habits of Highly Effective People*.

Samaritans – Charity founded in 1953. It provides telephone-based emotional support to people who are in distress or at risk of suicide.

Xian Zhang – Orchestra conductor. She was appointed the first female music director of an Italian symphony orchestra. In 2017, she became the first female conductor to conduct the BBC Proms.

Develop me

☜ Coach yourself

What do you enjoy most about listening intently to others?

How does your Listener strength help you most in your daily life and work activities?

In what situations is your Listener strength the most effective?

✓ Apply yourself

Expose yourself to listening to a variety of people so that you can support and learn from a diverse group rather than always the same people.

A customer facing role is calling you, whether this is internal or external. You will fully explore the customer's needs rather than offering a solution too quickly.

You are able to develop a deep understanding of people. Apply this knowledge to support any complex needs at home, with team members or those in your community.

⚠ Watch out for yourself

Know when to speak. Your strength in showing a keen interest in what others have to say can, if overplayed, stifle interpersonal communication. Communication is a two-way process – know when to shift from Listener to speaker to help maintain a smooth dialogue. Ensure you play an active role in what is going on.

Mission

Understand me

I derive great fulfilment from pursuing activities that give my life meaning and purpose. The focus of my purpose could be one or many different things, but whatever it is, I'm committed to pursuing it. How I spend my time, the decisions I make, and the plans I have for the future are all aligned to my overriding sense of Mission and purpose.

Describe me

"I try to follow my heart and do things that are worthwhile, giving a real sense of meaning to people's lives."

"I am committed to working for the benefit of others, to making their lives more enjoyable, and to make this sustainable."

"Making a difference is at the heart of everything I do."

"Working for the right organisation is far more important than my pay or benefits. I need to do what matters, because nothing else does."

"I enjoy sharing and communicating my mission so that others feel included. I make sure I remind myself to share in their passions too."

People like me

Matt Damon – Actor and co-founder of water.org. The charity provides access to safe water and sanitation with the purpose that "Every human being deserves to define their own future".

Bill and Melinda Gates – American philanthropists and humanitarians. They created the world's wealthiest charitable foundation and have pledged to eventually give away 95% of their wealth.

Dame Anita Roddick – British entrepreneur, environmentalist and founder of The Body Shop, the company that shaped ethical consumerism for cosmetic products.

Develop me

☺ Coach yourself

What do you believe to be your life's purpose?

What is driving you towards fulfilment of your life's Mission and purpose?

What activities do you do daily that work towards this Mission?

✓ Apply yourself

Get visual with your hopes, dreams, passions and goals. Create quotes and reminders for phones, desks, and fridges that will keep you motivated.

Share your Mission with others and enlist their support. Partner with those strong in Organiser or Action, or draw on your own Personal Responsibility. Turn dreams into reality.

Be clear with the business case of your Mission. Convey this with facts and a strong purpose. Opinions don't count when persuading others.

⚠ Watch out for yourself

Don't let your Mission be the only Mission. Your strength in aligning your plans, decisions and time according to your life purpose can, if overplayed, dominate everything you do. Flex your style and know when to contribute to helping others achieve their own life goals.

Moral Compass

Understand me

I'm a very moral person with an extremely strong ethical code. I'm very aware of the difference between right and wrong, and always act in accordance with what I believe is right. I'm clear on my values and my moral reasoning for what I do and why I do it.

Describe me

"My decisions and actions are always guided by my ethics and values, and I never step outside of these."

"I just have to do the right thing. I always stand by this as it's the only way to make decisions that affect people."

"My own personal position can become irrelevant. If there are consequences from me doing the right thing, then so be it."

"My friends know where they stand with me as I am very faithful and consistent. I have a clear view of what is acceptable."

"I can find it difficult to give and take on something I feel very strongly about. I've learned to see things from other angles."

People like me

Martin Bell OBE – Former BBC war reporter. He argued that the neutral reporting of armed conflicts did a disservice to viewers when it was clear that atrocities were being committed. He stood as an independent MP for the British Parliament to protest against 'sleaze' in politics.

Rosa Parks – African-American civil rights activist. She sparked the Montgomery Bus Boycott by refusing to give up her seat for a white passenger, which she did as a private citizen who was 'tired of giving in'.

Jeffrey Wigand – Former Vice President of Research and Development at tobacco company Brown & Williamson. He is renowned as a whistle-blower who shared insight into harmful industry practices with the public when he appeared on the CBS news programme, *60 Minutes.*

Develop me

☝ Coach yourself

Where does your strength of acting in keeping with your values come from?

How does your Moral Compass strength guide your day-to-day actions and decisions?

Of which moral action or decision are you most proud?

✓ Apply yourself

Surround yourself with people who share similar values to you at work and at home. Work together to strengthen your values and find ways to channel your beliefs.

Communicate what's important to you and adapt your approach to suit your audience. Those around you need to know what you believe, but do not need to be preached at.

Be a role model around sensitive issues and subjects. Encourage others to listen, understand, not judge, and act in the right way.

⚠ Watch out for yourself

Don't be righteous. Your strength in being clear on your values and moral code can, if overplayed, lead you to judge others strictly by your own standards. Not everyone will live their life by the same values and moral code as you do. Be open to learning what is important to others.

Narrator

Understand me

I have a tremendous love of story. Even as ordinary events happen, I can picture how they might be spun into an anecdote or story for me to tell others. I love to answer questions in the form of a story. I can always see the power of stories to convey morals, insights, values, humour and other lessons to people.

Describe me

"For me, life is one big story waiting to be told. It comes so naturally to me, I don't even notice I'm telling a story."

"I often use stories as a way of relating to people. I encourage them to share their own, so I can store them up to tell others later."

"I find I can engage an audience easily as I take a concept or fact and then take people on a journey of its importance."

"I'm always using my own experiences to make people laugh. It works much better than a joke and they remember the point of the story."

"When time is limited, I must remember to keep my stories short or get to the point."

People like me

Sir David Attenborough – A veteran English broadcaster and naturalist. His career in broadcasting has stretched over more than half a century and has become known as the face and voice of natural history documentaries.

Walt Disney – American film producer. He had the ability to immerse you in his stories and create an experience, gaining 22 Oscars across his works.

J.K. Rowling – International best-selling author. She wrote the *Harry Potter* fantasy series and has sold more than 500 million copies of her books worldwide in 80 languages.

Develop me

⚬ Coach yourself

What was the last effective story you told to deliver an important message?

How do you go about creating your stories?

In what situations does your Narrator strength work best for you?

✓ Apply yourself

You will be at your best in roles where you have an audience and something compelling to say. Avoid the back office.

Not every story needs to be your own. Encourage the sharing of stories and adapt them for your audience.

Consider the variety of ways to tell a story. Try social media, blogs, a quote, or a picture to give yourself a break from a long verbal or written performance.

⚠ Watch out for yourself

Don't become a story bore. Your strength in using stories and anecdotes to relate everyday events and answer questions can, if overplayed, be wearing for others. Know when a short or succinct response will be more appropriate than a lengthy narrative or story.

Optimism

Understand me

I always see the best side of any situation, with a consistent and firm belief that things will work out well in the future. Having this belief keeps me strong and enables me to stay positive even when things are difficult.

Describe me

"I always look on the bright side of life. I just hate being miserable."

"I often find that people around me complain about things more than I do. I don't see the point, you have to make the best of the situation you're in."

"I usually bring everyone else's positive spirits up, as I'm told my positivity can be contagious."

"In life there will always be challenges, so it's important to think positive and that's what I always do."

"I have had to learn that there are occasions when it's better to acknowledge sadness or disappointment, rather than being upbeat all the time."

People like me

Anne Frank – Dutch Jew. She famously hid with her family in a secret attic until they were discovered and sent to concentration camps, the horrors of which are shared in her diary, *The Diary of Anne Frank*.

Walter Hagen – American professional golf player. He was famously quoted as saying "Don't forget to stop and smell the roses".

Dilma Rousseff – Brazilian economist and politician. She served as the 36th President of Brazil and famously quoted "I hope the fathers and mothers of little girls will look at them and say 'Yes, women can'".

Develop me

⚙ Coach yourself

What enables you to always maintain a positive outlook?

What impact does your Optimism have on you or on those around you?

How do you bring others around to your positive way of viewing situations?

✓ Apply yourself

Add some unplanned positivity into your relationships. Arrange something unexpected to lift the mood, send a note of encouragement, or celebrate something small.

Share with others the valid reasons for your hope and Optimism to avoid you coming across as naive. Reality combined with positivity will be very influential.

Your positive outlook will focus people. Work on more difficult projects to keep spirits high, or help others see what they have learned after challenging tasks.

⚠ Watch out for yourself

Don't be unrealistic. Your strength in expecting things to work out for the best can, if overplayed, lead you to have unrealistic expectations or miss problems. Natural Optimism will help you persevere but there are times when it is necessary to give up – failure can also be an important experience.

Organiser

Understand me

I love to be exceptionally well-organised. Everything has its place, both in my work and my personal life. My order and organisation mean that I'm able to be as effective as possible in everything I do. I always know where things are, what to do when, and why something is important.

Describe me

"I firmly believe that everything has its place. When it doesn't, nothing delights me more than to find a place for it."

"In all areas of my life, I like things to be organised. It helps me focus on what I need to do, knowing where everything is."

"I get really excited when I am asked to organise something that is a complete mess. It is so satisfying to see the end result."

"My friends often rely on me for events and socials, as I think of everything and everyone to make it successful."

"I have learnt not everyone loves to be organised, so I try to help where I can without taking over, however hard this is!"

People like me

David Beckham OBE – Former British footballer and businessman. He has shared in interviews his need for order, reportedly with a colour coded fridge and even number of drinks.

A.A. Milne – Author of *Winnie the Pooh*. He is quoted as saying "Organising is what you do before you do something, so that when you do it, it is not all mixed up".

Abraham Ortelius – Flemish cartographer. He is generally recognised as the creator of the first modern atlas.

Develop me

☺ Coach yourself

How does your strength in Organiser reveal itself in your life?

How does being organised help you achieve your daily tasks at home and at work?

In what situation has your Organiser strength been the most effective?

✓ Apply yourself

Communicate your desire for order rather than inflexibility. Let people know you work more efficiently with deadlines, priorities and structure, and how to approach this with you.

What routines can you create at home or at work that will ease any frustrations? Make order easily accessible for others so they can join in.

Remember, others may reach success in a different way. Learn to give tips, help along structure, share your best templates and then take a step back.

⚠ Watch out for yourself

Know when to allow disorder. Your strength in having a place for everything can, if overplayed, come across as overly constraining to others. Not everyone enjoys structure and order. Be prepared to relax your focus to engage others – and be open to new information or ideas.

Persistence

Understand me

I pride myself on being able to keep going in the face of difficult challenges, frustrations and seemingly insurmountable problems. I understand that success in the face of adversity requires extra effort and determination, so I never give up.

Describe me

"It's deeply instilled in me to never, ever give up. I've achieved many things with this mantra."

"I often find others around me giving up on a task way before I do, if I ever do."

"I've been called a dog with a bone sometimes; I just love the feeling of finding a way forward when it seemed there wasn't one."

"I don't give up on people. We all make mistakes and friendships are too important to let go."

"I've learned when to give up on an argument, and that not everyone will always see my point of view on ways forward."

People like me

Eddie Izzard – British comedian. He ran 27 marathons in 27 days as a tribute to the 27 years Nelson Mandela spent in prison.

Dame Ellen MacArthur – British sailor. She broke the world record for fastest solo circumnavigation of the world in a sea craft.

Cha Sa-Soon – Korean woman. She passed her driving theory test on her 950th time – taking 2 buses and a train every week day until she passed.

Develop me

⚙ Coach yourself

What drives you to keep going when things are challenging?

Which situation are you most proud of for maintaining your Persistence?

What strategies do you use to maintain your Persistence?

✓ Apply yourself

Consider roles or tasks in a customer facing environment. You will be excellent in resolving a customer's complex issues patiently, no matter what they throw at you.

Keep others motivated during tougher or longer-term projects. Explain your rationale for keeping going. Be a role model to stay future-focused.

Partner with those strong in Judgement or Strategic Awareness to ensure you are working on the right approach. Your focus should be on the successful end goal, not simply keeping going.

⚠ Watch out for yourself

Know when to give up. Your strength in achieving success by pushing yourself on can, if overplayed, be misguided. Balance your Persistence with an ability to judge when to let go and focus your efforts elsewhere. Sometimes, withdrawal is the better option than Persistence.

Personal Responsibility

Understand me

I'm always true to my word. If I make a promise or commitment, then I make sure that I keep it. I never blame others but take ownership of everything I do and hold myself accountable for doing it. I'm seen as someone who is always prepared to do what I have promised.

Describe me

"My friends and family know that they can always count on me. Letting them down isn't an option."

"I always keep promises to people, no matter what. It's really important to me that I deliver what I say, when I say it."

"I work best when I am being held accountable and own the task, however big or small. I enjoy responsibility."

"If I ever make a mistake it feels awful. I always own up to it and immediately see what I can do to put it right."

"I do need to be patient and appreciate that others don't always want as much responsibility as me."

People like me

Viktor Frankl – Austrian psychiatrist and Holocaust survivor. He once recommended that the "Statue of Liberty [on the East Coast] be supplemented by a Statue of Responsibility on the West Coast".

Captain Lawrence Oates – Antarctic hero and explorer. He walked out to his deliberate death so as not to hold up Scott of the Antarctic on the expedition to the South Pole.

Irena Sendler – Polish Catholic social worker. She served in the Polish Underground during the Second World War and saved more than 2,500 Jewish children by smuggling them out of the Warsaw ghetto.

Develop me

☺ Coach yourself

What types of activities do you find yourself consistently taking responsibility for?

What do you love most about taking responsibility for things upon yourself?

Are there ever situations you are unable to take responsibility for? How do you feel when this happens?

✓ Apply yourself

You won't take too kindly to be being told what to do all day, so take on roles and tasks where you have autonomy and can report back on your successes.

Take on sections of larger complex projects at work or home. Be clear on what you will do as part of this and lead your own priorities for the agreed timescales.

Take on things you don't normally do and for different people. Stretch yourself in different ways using your strengths, finding your own way to deliver on them.

⚠ Watch out for yourself

Don't beat yourself up. Your strength in always following through on your commitments can, if overplayed, impact negatively on your wellbeing and relationships. Allow others to take responsibility and learn to balance your promises with the other important things in life.

Personalisation

Understand me

I notice the subtle differences in people that make them unique. I recognise the different motivators of individual people, as well as their likes, dislikes, preferences, strengths and talents. I love to relate to everyone as a unique individual, recognising that what is right for one person may not be right for another.

Describe me

"I pick up on the differences in people. I know that to get the best out of a person, you need to treat them as an individual."

"I focus really carefully on people's needs and then direct my attention accordingly. People always seem surprised with what I pick up from this."

"Everyone has unique capabilities. I enjoy taking my time to get to know what these are and appreciate them. It brings a smile to people's faces."

"We all want to be remembered for what we bring. I love that I can tap into this by giving people tasks that match their strengths."

"I find I need to point out my own strengths and weaknesses to other people, rather than assuming they know what they are."

People like me

Katharine Cook Briggs – Co-creator of the Myers-Briggs Type Indicator® (MBTI). Together with her daughter, she was an astute observer of human behaviour and individual differences.

John Paul DeJoria – Self-made billionaire and co-founder of the Paul Mitchell line of hair products. His staff turnover is fewer than 100 people after 37 years, attributed to the way their needs are catered for.

Carl Gustav Jung – Swiss psychologist. He originated the theory of psychological types, arguing that every person follows their own individual path of personal growth and development.

Develop me

⚙ Coach yourself

Where does your strength in relating to people as unique individuals come from?

What is it that you do that enables you to personalise your approach so successfully with each different person?

How do you use this strength to support your daily tasks?

✓ Apply yourself

Get involved more in mentoring, coaching, teaching, training, sales or customer service. Your Personalisation will see your audience at ease and help them enjoy relating to you.

As well as noting and appreciating people's uniqueness, ensure you set tasks in the areas of their strengths. Keep developing and challenging their individuality.

Help new people fit in through friendship groups or teams. Introduce them to others by way of their special qualities.

⚠ Watch out for yourself

Don't over-personalise. Your strength in valuing each person as a unique individual can, if overplayed, mean that you miss what people have in common. Learn when it may be helpful to point out commonalities, or when people need to experience something other than their uniqueness.

Persuasion

Understand me

I'm particularly effective at convincing others and bringing them around to my point of view. I love to make a good argument for what I want, choosing my language, words, and methods carefully to win agreement from others.

Describe me

"When I require a different approach by someone, I get them to see how good the idea is themselves through their own suggestions or research."

"I find one of the best ways to get someone on board with my ideas is to help them take ownership of it themselves."

"Reality and a business case is critical in convincing someone to do something they don't want to do. I always know my facts."

"People follow along with me quite easily. I'm seen as a good leader as I'm confident enough to ask people for what I would like."

"I'm conscious not to push others into something they don't want to do. I don't want to break their trust."

People like me

Baroness Karren Brady CBE – Former Managing Director of Birmingham City Football Club and entrepreneur. She persuaded David Sullivan to let her buy and run the Club, becoming the first woman to hold the post in the top flight of English football, and the youngest managing director of a UK plc.

Og Mandino – American author. He wrote *The Greatest Salesman in the World*, containing the 'time-tested wisdom of the ancients distilled into ten simple scrolls'.

Franklin D. Roosevelt – 32nd US President. In his first 'fireside chat' on radio, he restored stability in the banking system and gave America much needed hope and calm.

Develop me

⚅ Coach yourself

What energises you most about bringing other people round to your way of thinking?

What do you do to persuade others successfully?

In what situations do you use this strength most effectively?

✓ Apply yourself

Be clear with others about the intentions and passions for your persuasiveness. You don't want to be seen simply as arguing, but instead as fighting for a good cause.

Build positive relationships around you, as you never know when you might need people's vote. Make conversations two way – get to know people and build their trust.

You are likely to prefer action and can be direct. Surround yourself with people who can build the plan, understand the challenges, and be compassionate about any consequences.

⚠ Watch out for yourself

Make sure your way is the right way. Your strength in making a good case for what you want can, if overplayed, result in you defending or promoting something that you shouldn't. Learn to judge when to step back from being persuasive – perhaps when there are more effective alternatives.

Planner

31

Understand me

I have a natural ability to plan and prepare, taking a deliberate and systematic approach to everything I do. Before starting things I think carefully, get organised, establish time frames, and assess and allocate resources. I love to make sure that I have covered all eventualities – including planning for the unexpected.

Describe me

"For me, it's essential to have a plan before I do anything – I work much better that way. My friendships are quite organised too."

"I just love organising events. I put a lot of time and effort into the planning stage because I feel that it is the only way to guarantee success."

"I plan well in advance of any deadline, so I have plenty of time to deal with the unexpected and be satisfied with all the details."

"I make sure that I plan everything to the very last detail, so that nothing is left to chance."

"I can find it quite difficult when working with someone who hates planning. I usually find there is a balance to be had."

People like me

Le Corbusier – Swiss-French architect. He was a pioneer of modern architecture who designed Chandigarh, the first planned city in India, famous for its architecture and urban planning.

George Marshall – Nobel Peace Prize recipient and US Secretary of State. He was the architect of the Marshall Plan for the post-war reconstruction of Europe after the Second World War.

Marina Raskova – Soviet aviator. She was the first woman to become a navigator in the Soviet Air Force and is the holder of several long distance flight records, for one of which she was decorated with the Hero of the Soviet Union.

Develop me

☞ Coach yourself

How have you made the greatest difference by being your most systematic?

What is it that most energises you about planning?

How do others benefit from your plans?

✓ Apply yourself

You love a good deadline, so insist on your tasks and projects having a deadline – or set yourself one. Share your step-by-step plan to achieve this when other people are involved.

You may find it useful to work with someone who loves spontaneity and creativity. This will build flexibility and fresh ideas into your plans, as well as meeting the deadline.

Stick to roles with structure. Sell your dependency, discipline, and above all efficiency to people. Challenge others for more detail when they give you a task, to help your performance.

⚠ Watch out for yourself

Know when to be spontaneous. Your strength in taking a systematic approach to everything you do can, if overplayed, mean you will rarely relax. Learn to spot when a plan is not necessary, so that you can try being enthusiastic and open to spontaneous suggestions.

Prevention

Understand me

I love to think ahead and anticipate problems before they happen. I notice the little things that might be out of place or going wrong, and then deal with them. I notice, where others may not, the areas that need attention to prevent future problems.

Describe me

"I believe we can stop a lot of things happening if we consider and plan out tasks and projects properly in advance."

"Whatever task I undertake, I'm always on the lookout for challenges and hidden issues. Then I like to make sure that I do something so that they don't happen."

"I look around the house some days and think 'It's an accident waiting to happen'. If I didn't act on my suspicions, I know that they would play on my mind."

"I try to anticipate future problems in my relationships by being as open as possible. It's better to stop any issues escalating."

"I have learnt that some things you can't pre-empt. I'm often teased that I can't control the weather."

People like me

Sir Alexander Fleming – Recipient of the Nobel Prize in Medicine. He discovered penicillin, which has since been used as an antibiotic in the treatment and prevention of a wide range of infections and illnesses.

Kylie Minogue – Australian actress and singer. After speaking openly about her breast cancer diagnosis and battle, she encouraged other young women to have regular checks, creating the 'Kylie effect'.

Dame Stella Rimington – Director-General of MI5. She was the first woman to hold the post at the British Security Service from 1992-1996.

Develop me

◌ Coach yourself

What drives you to focus on anticipating problems and dealing with them before they happen?

What resources do you draw on to ensure you always judge situations, and your subsequent interventions, correctly?

How do you use your ability to anticipate and prevent problems daily in your tasks?

✓ Apply yourself

Always explain your rationale for caution, so as not to look too timid or fearful of action. While your instincts are usually right, back them up with some calculated risks.

Rather than take on all the responsibility, carve out a role for yourself as a sounding board on home and work initiatives. Come up with the ideas, not always the plan.

When something goes wrong, help people review what happened and what could have been prevented. Identify warning signs and ideas to ensure it doesn't happen again.

⚠ Watch out for yourself

Don't forget to live a little. Your strength in thinking ahead can, if overplayed, hinder your ability to enjoy yourself or act spontaneously. Be attuned to when you need to relax your focus. Be prepared to take a risk every now and then – it's good for you and will help to keep you fresh.

Pride

Understand me

I take Pride in everything that I do. I love to consistently deliver work that is of the highest standard and quality, getting it right first time, every time. I set high standards for myself and enjoy others' recognition for the quality of what I do.

Describe me

"'Only the best will do' is an attitude that I apply to all my work – it's the only way."

"I'm often considered a perfectionist, but it's just that I consider high quality to be important in everything."

"Whatever I am working on, I like to make it the best it can be, rather than settle just for what was asked of me."

"I love to receive praise for a job well done. If I don't receive this praise, I find myself evaluating what could have made it even better."

"I can get frustrated when my friends and colleagues are a little sloppy in their approach."

People like me

Dame Judi Dench – British actress. She has won numerous awards, is a seven-time Oscar nominee, and has more than once been named number one in polls for Britain's best actor.

Lewis Hamilton MBE – A four-time Formula One racing driver World Champion. He is considered the best driver of his generation and widely regarded as one of the greatest Formula One drivers of all time.

Donatella Versace – Italian fashion designer and VP of the Versace Group. She has been credited by Google as the reason Google Images was created, since so many people searched for her iconic 'Grammy dress' worn by Jennifer Lopez.

The Strengths Profile Book

Develop me

☞ Coach yourself

Where does your enjoyment of delivering work of the highest quality come from?

What does your focus on quality achieve for you and for others?

How do you ensure that the quality you strive to deliver is appropriate for its context?

✓ Apply yourself

Even if it is not to your standard, be more appreciative of the effort of others, however small the task. Encouraging quality will see more of it.

What tools do you use to ensure your own quality? Share your tips and encourage people to work together to ensure a higher standard in their work.

Don't make assumptions. Make it clear what you would like the result to look like, giving examples.

⚠ Watch out for yourself

Don't be unreasonable. Your strength in setting high standards for yourself can, if overplayed, make you a harsh critic. Try not to dismiss the contributions of others. Encourage people, teach them, and try to find ways to get the best from them. Everyone has a contribution to make.

Rapport Builder

Understand me

I start conversations with people quickly and easily, including those I am meeting for the first time. I quickly find something that is of interest to us both, then open up the conversation further. I enjoy meeting people for the first time and getting to know them.

Describe me

"I just seem to be able to talk to anybody, at any time, about anything."

"My friends think it's funny that I can interact with quiet people easily and get people to smile who otherwise never seem to."

"For me, the starting point of connecting with people is about engaging with them in a way that's comfortable and enjoyable."

"I enjoy meeting strangers and finding common interests and experiences that we can talk about."

"I'm mindful that there are times when I need to invest a bit more in a relationship, other than just making the first meeting great."

People like me

Mo Mowlam – British Secretary of State for Northern Ireland. She oversaw the signing of the historic Good Friday Peace Agreement in 1998 and had a reputation for plain speaking.

Sir Michael Parkinson – British chat show host. He is known as the 'great British talk show host' and was knighted for his services to broadcasting.

Anwar Sadat – Former President of Egypt. He received the Nobel Peace Prize and was the first leader of an Arab league nation to make a treaty with Israel.

Develop me

Coach yourself

What motivates you to get to know people?

What makes you so effective at building rapport with others?

Are there any situations where you find it more challenging to build rapport with people? Why is this?

Apply yourself

You love to meet new people, so don't get stuck behind a desk all day – or make sure you have a very sociable hobby. Put new people at ease, charm clients and build your future networks.

As you build your many connections, jot down in your phone something unique about them. Bring this up the next time you meet them, to start to forge deeper relationships.

People will see you as friendly, engaging and warm. Play to this and enjoy two-way conversations, rather than bombarding people with too many questions.

Watch out for yourself

Know when to step back. Your strength in building relationships easily with others can, if overplayed, be perceived by others as inauthentic or intrusive. Some people develop relationships at a slower pace, over time – be sure to give them the time they need to do this.

Relationship Deepener

Understand me

Building close relationships with people is very important to me. For me, really getting to know someone and for them to know me takes time. My relationships with people will develop slowly but nearly always last over the long term.

Describe me

"I have made a number of friends over the years and I love keeping in contact with them. A friend is a friend for life."

"Even if I meet up with a colleague I haven't seen for some time, it's like a day hasn't passed since I saw them."

"If I am visiting a friend or client, I try to pop in and see another friend or client in the area, even if it's just for a quick coffee."

"Keeping my relationships alive and developing them further is very important to me. You never know when you will need them."

"I tend to connect with others on all levels, intellectual and emotional, but I find it harder to make relationships based on small talk."

People like me

Athos, Porthos and Aramis – The Three Musketeers of Alexandre Dumas' novel. They live by the motto "All for one and one for all".

Herbert and Zelmyra Fisher – Guinness World Record for the longest marriage of a living couple. They were married for 86 years and when asked for their secret, said "With each day that passed, our relationship was more solid and secure".

Nelson Mandela – Former President of South Africa. He was the key negotiator in ending the apartheid regime in South Africa, partly achieved through his relationship with white President F.W. De Clerk. They were both jointly awarded the Nobel Peace Prize as a result.

Develop me

⚙ Coach yourself

What are some of the relationships in which you have found fulfilment through investing your time?

How do you know which relationships to invest in?

How do you like to keep in touch and build the relationships with the people you are close to?

✓ Apply yourself

Make time to invest in new relationships as well as continuing to build on existing ones. Be sociable outside of work and only invest in the most rewarding relationships.

Take on roles where building trust is important, perhaps disgruntled clients or new friends with problems. You'll get to know them and the issues they face, figuring out where you can be of help.

Review the diversity of your friendships. Are they all the same age and mix in the same circles, or can you encourage a more diverse group that you can learn from?

⚠ Watch out for yourself

Know when to back off. Your strength in building deep and lasting relationships with people can, if overplayed, mean you direct your efforts inappropriately. Learn to gauge when others require a less intimate approach or when connecting with someone at a more superficial level will be of benefit.

Resilience

Understand me

I have a terrific ability to overcome adversity. I take hardships and setbacks in my stride. I always find the resources and strength to pick myself back up, even in the most difficult circumstances. I know that I have the strength to cope with, and recover from, anything that life throws at me.

Describe me

"You can't keep me down for long. There's no point. 'Learn from it and move on', that's what I say."

"When my suggestions get knocked back, I don't give up. I find another way to keep on track and get people to listen."

"I've had achievements in my life and these have all happened because I kept going when others would have given up."

"I've had my fair share of challenges, but it seems to have made me stronger and better able to cope with things."

"I do get hurt on occasions. There are times I should probably show this more to my friends and colleagues."

People like me

Thomas Edison – American inventor. He was the holder of 1,093 US patents and is most famous as the inventor of the practical electric light bulb – despite having failed 1,000 times in his attempts to do so.

Helen Keller – American author and activist. She was the first deaf and blind woman to earn a college degree and went on to a prolific writing career.

Dame Jane Tomlinson – British amateur athlete. Despite being diagnosed with terminal cancer, she raised £1.85 million for charity through a series of athletic challenges, including completing the London Marathon three times and cycling across both Europe and the United States.

Develop me

Coach yourself

When was the first time you noticed your ability to pick yourself up from a tough situation?

What enables you to maintain your Resilience through challenging circumstances?

When has your Resilience been most tested to the extreme?

Apply yourself

Be a role model on the road to recovery. Talk openly and warmly about your challenges and the strategies you use for overcoming them. Inspire others to keep going.

Support people through times of change. Give them the optimism of the end outcome and continue giving them hope along the way if they encounter challenges.

Rest your Resilience sometimes. This allows people to get to know the real you and what makes you vulnerable, but also ensures you don't get tired from the perpetual struggle.

Watch out for yourself

Don't become too hardened. Your strength in taking hardships and setbacks in your stride can, if overplayed, become something you take an inappropriate level of pride in. Learn to balance your Resilience with an ability to engage as an equal and show humility where necessary.

Resolver

Understand me

I love solving problems, the more complicated the problem, the better. I thrive on getting my teeth into a really complex problem and focusing on getting to the root of it, whatever it might be. I will always go the extra mile to find a solution, being extremely thorough, and pursuing all avenues to get a good result.

Describe me

"In my view, every problem has a solution. Nothing gives me greater pleasure than trying to find it."

"I'm rarely beaten by a problem and I love it when I beat a particularly challenging one. I seem to hear the word 'problem' a mile off."

"I find I'm always getting involved in helping and advising on any problem, it just comes naturally to me to get involved."

"People always come to me for advice on approaches to different situations. I can usually help unlock them, even if it isn't an area I know much about."

"I've learned that sometimes, despite me wanting to fix it, a problem doesn't need to be fixed. I just have to be patient."

People like me

Archimedes – One of the greatest mathematicians of all time. He famously cried "Eureka!" when he stepped into a bath and noticed that the water level rose, solving how to calculate the volume of irregular objects, a previously intractable problem.

Violeta Chamorro – Former President of Nicaragua. She was the first elected female head of government in Latin America. Her election and policies helped to end Nicaragua's eleven-year civil war.

Ada, Countess of Lovelace – English mathematician. She was known as the first computer programmer for her work on Charles Babbage's mechanical general-purpose computer.

Develop me

⚜ Coach yourself

What is it about problem solving that you particularly enjoy?

When you think about the problems you have most successfully solved, which are you most proud of?

How do you approach solving challenging problems?

✓ Apply yourself

Keep up-to-date with the latest technology surrounding your area of expertise. Be at the ready to solve issues more quickly when they arise.

Partner with someone with the Prevention strength or dial up your own. There may be times when you could have helped anticipate the issue before it happened.

Don't rush in with resolving problems. Consider all the options and the people involved. Try to enable others along the way rather than always being the go-to person.

⚠ Watch out for yourself

Know when to give up. Your strength in getting to the root of problems can, if overplayed, take its toll on your wellbeing and relationships. Learn to spot when a problem cannot be solved or is impacting negatively on other important things. Keep perspective on when to persevere and when to withdraw.

Self-awareness

Understand me

I enjoy spending time and focusing effort on understanding my behaviour, emotions and responses to different situations. I have a deep awareness and understanding of my strengths and weaknesses. By having this Self-awareness, my behaviour doesn't surprise me or catch me off guard.

Describe me

"I live in a very self-reflective way and know my limits, abilities and preferences very well."

"I often question myself and my motives as I'm aware of what I'm doing, how I might be perceived, and the way I come across."

"I find I have authentic relationships as I'm really happy to change, grow and accept feedback. I do this better than most other people."

"Knowing myself as I do helps me to be more open to knowing others. I love to find out others' strengths and weaknesses too."

"My friends have told me to relax and to just enjoy the moment, rather than worrying all the time about how I might sound."

People like me

Kate Adie CBE – British journalist. She is best known for reporting from war zones around the world. Her career was launched when she was the first on scene to report live on the London Iranian Embassy siege in 1980.

Robert De Niro – American actor, film director, and producer. He has won many awards including two Academy Awards and is recognised for his ability to translate himself into the characters he is playing.

Bruce Lee – Chinese American martial artist and actor. He was considered by many to be the most influential martial artist of the 20th century and a cultural icon.

Develop me

⚙ Coach yourself

How has your knowledge of your emotions and behaviour developed over time?

How do you use your Self-awareness to support daily tasks?

What strategies do you use to build and maintain a high level of Self-awareness?

✓ Apply yourself

Ask for feedback from people you might not initially be tempted to ask, maybe at home or in different teams. They may see you differently. Develop what they love about you even further.

Take on more of a learning role in your world. Help others to spot their strengths and weaknesses and allocate tasks accordingly.

Encourage a feedback environment at home and at work. People may avoid both positive and negative feedback, so encourage everyone to spot and encourage greatness.

⚠ Watch out for yourself

Don't become self-obsessed. Your strength in committing time and effort to understanding yourself better can, if overplayed, be perceived as self-indulgent. Balance your focus on yourself with a sufficient focus on others, or on the situation or task at hand.

Self-belief

Understand me

I'm very confident and self-assured, with a firm belief in my own strengths and abilities. With this self-confidence, I always believe that I can achieve the goals I am working towards. I believe that almost anything is within my reach if I set my mind to it and work hard to achieve it.

Describe me

"I have a 'can do' attitude to life. If you don't try, then you will never know what you could have achieved."

"I find that my self-belief instils a confidence in the people around me, which is very satisfying."

"I know that I am good at influencing, so I'm often asked to speak up or manage situations that others don't want to."

"I never think I am going to fail when I go into a situation. I've usually done my homework so I'm comfortable to go and get on with it."

"I never want to come across as arrogant with my confidence, so there are some people where I play it down a bit."

People like me

Joan of Arc – National heroine of France and a Catholic saint. Legend has it that she led a French army as a teenager during the Hundred Years War, and she was ultimately burned at the stake at the age of just 19.

Lee Kuan Yew – First Prime Minister of Singapore. He was credited with building the jungle island into an Asian financial capital and transitioning the country from the 'third world to first world in a single generation' under his leadership.

Oprah Winfrey – American billionaire, talk show host and actress. Best known for her talk show *The Oprah Winfrey Show*, the highest-rated television programme of its kind in history, she is often described as the most influential woman in the world.

Develop me

☞ Coach yourself

Where does your confidence in your ability to do things come from?

What enables you to maintain and sustain your belief in your own abilities?

In what situation has your Self-belief been most challenged?

✐ Apply yourself

Lead, sell and persuade. Try these skills in a new social setting or work environment where you see a gap. Adapt your approach to different audiences.

Consider your other strengths and explore how your Self-belief can elevate these and stretch you further. Is there any goal that you still shy away from?

Be a role model of confidence. Take ownership of difficult conversations or situations, and guide others to solutions when there is confusion.

⚠ Watch out for yourself

Don't be arrogant. Your strength in believing that you can achieve most things can, if overplayed, be judged by others as arrogant. Learn to monitor how you come across to others, and balance your confidence with a degree of humility where appropriate.

Service

Understand me

I feel compelled to help people as much as I can. I get a great deal of satisfaction when I have helped someone. I strive to go above and beyond what I need to do, often exceeding people's expectations. I'm focused entirely on satisfying people's needs and meeting their requirements.

Describe me

"Nothing is too much trouble. I really love to help people and I just can't stop myself from doing it."

"People are often surprised by the level of help I provide. If you need a plaster, I'll arrive with a first aid kit and I'm on hand for the hospital."

"I take time to listen to people's needs, get any information they need, sort immediate problems out, and then often come back to them to check if there is anything else."

"People appreciate me for what I do for them but if they didn't, I would do it anyway, I just can't help helping!"

"I have been known to be helping quite a few people on the go at the same time. I usually need a bit of a rest after this."

People like me

Clara Barton – American nurse in the Civil War. She founded the American Red Cross, provided self-taught nursing care and was a keen humanitarian.

Prince Philip, Duke of Edinburgh – Founded the Duke of Edinburgh's Award (DofE) in 1956, transforming the lives of millions of young people through valuable life experiences.

Florence Nightingale – British nurse, famous for her service during the Crimean War where she was known as 'The Lady with the Lamp' for tending injured soldiers through the night. Her book *Notes on Nursing* became the foundation for professional nursing, and International Nurses Day recognises her birthday.

Develop me

☺ Coach yourself

When did your strength in helping others first come to the fore?

In what situations and with whom are you the happiest when helping others?

How do you decide who to reach out to and go the extra mile for?

✓ Apply yourself

Consider the customer journey where you work. What is the customer's feedback or experience of your business? Help with ideas to improve the Service provided.

Don't take it all upon yourself. Create a culture in your friendships and workplace where it is okay to ask for help, and people know where to go and who to ask to get it.

As you support others, enable them along the way so they can learn ready for next time. Otherwise you may be permanently on call, and restricted in who else you can help.

⚠ Watch out for yourself

Don't forget yourself. Your strength in supporting others on a regular basis can, if overplayed, affect your wellbeing. Avoid becoming so focused on attending to others' needs that you miss meeting your own. Serving others well means ensuring your own needs are sufficiently catered for too.

Spotlight

Understand me

I enjoy being the centre of attention. Whether in a meeting or in a social gathering, I naturally speak up and hold the floor. I like holding people's interest and focus. I can get people to listen to me and keep their attention – whatever else might be going on.

Describe me

"Performing and talking is what I am all about. I just love being the centre of attention and having people looking at me."

"I get a real buzz from being listened to. I try to do this in an engaging way, so others enjoy what I have to say."

"Any opportunity I get, I entertain people and make them laugh through stories, experiences, and jokes."

"I am often more comfortable with public speaking or speaking in large groups, than I am with a one-to-one conversation."

"I'm conscious not to take over and steal the limelight as other people need to share their views, although this can be difficult!"

People like me

Sir Richard Branson – Founder of Virgin Group. He has attempted many world records and events, including the fastest crossing of the Atlantic Ocean by both boat and hot air balloon, the fastest crossing of the Pacific Ocean by hot air balloon, and the fastest crossing of the English Channel in an amphibious vehicle.

Madonna – American singer. She has been recognised as the best-selling female recording artist of all time by the Guinness Book of World Records and is reported to have sold over 300 million albums.

Oscar Wilde – Irish playwright and poet. He wrote numerous short stories and one novel, being famous for his biting wit. He was one of the greatest celebrities of his day.

Develop me

Coach yourself

What underpins your desire to put yourself in the Spotlight?

What do you enjoy about speaking up in front of others?

How do you use your Spotlight strength to achieve your objectives?

Apply yourself

Presenting doesn't come naturally to most people. Find ways to partner with others, where they come up with the ideas and strategies and you deliver them or co-present.

Attend to your audience and adapt your presentation style. Rely on a range of tools like stories, videos and other presenters, rather than having it as just you speaking.

As well as how you say it, know what to say when. Ensure your contributions are relevant and timely, and your content is well-informed.

Watch out for yourself

Allow others their time in the Spotlight as well. Your strength in speaking up can, if overplayed, be at the expense of others. Encourage others to contribute their thoughts, views and ideas. Inclusion is critical in a team or organisational context.

Strategic Awareness

Understand me

I have a keen interest in understanding changes in the wider world that could impact on my plans and objectives. This big picture awareness enables me to develop and shift long-term plans effectively. I love to take steps to deal with whatever circumstances might arise in the future.

Describe me

"I'm always asking myself and others 'What does it mean for us?'"

"I love to think about what the future may bring. I try to picture what might be coming and what this means for my plans."

"I watch the news, read informed comments, study industry journals, track trends and pay attention to anomalies to inform my thinking."

"I have a view on what's going to happen next on topics and what it means for me, my home life, and my work. It isn't always 100% accurate, but my theme is generally right."

"Whilst I enjoy the bigger picture, I know that sometimes I need to focus on the smaller details too."

People like me

Catherine II (the Great) – Empress of Russia. She was the country's longest-ruling female leader, from 1762 until 1796. Under her rule, Russia was revitalised through several complex foreign policy successes and improved administration.

Dame Marjorie Scardino – American-born British executive. She was the first female CEO of a FTSE-100 company and is recognised for her Strategic Awareness and business acumen. In 2013 she joined the board of Twitter as its first female director.

Sun Tzu – 6th century BCE Chinese philosopher and General to the King of Wu. He wrote *The Art of War* on the basis of his military successes, regarded as the leading text on strategy.

Develop me

☻ Coach yourself

What do you enjoy about focusing on the bigger picture?

How do you apply your strategic mindset daily?

What is your biggest achievement using your Strategic Awareness strength?

✓ Apply yourself

You have great ideas, so consider sharing these outside your usual environment. Inject future thinking across different groups, cultures and charities.

Your future vision may seem like you are questioning or objecting to others' ideas, who are focused in the here and now. Explain your rationale and evidence, as well as the thinking behind your suggestions.

Partner up with others with strengths in Action, Planner and Resolver to execute your ideas and deliver on the more immediate milestones toward achievement.

⚠ Watch out for yourself

Don't over-strategise. Your strength in focusing only on the bigger picture can, if overplayed, result in practical realities being ignored. Spot when the shift needs to be made from strategy to planning, detail and practicalities. Strategic thinking is just daydreaming when it doesn't lead to deliverable action.

Time Optimiser

Understand me

Time is very precious to me and I never waste it. I love to squeeze as much as I can into every minute of every day, organising myself so that I use my time wisely and productively. Whatever situation I'm in, I make the most of my time.

Describe me

"I'm always thinking 'What can I be doing at this moment to make the best use of my time?'"

"It frustrates me to be waiting around for anything. I wish everyone could operate at the same speed as me."

"I would much prefer to do something rather than think or talk about something. You achieve so much more this way."

"Wasting time is not an option for me. I'll be tidying up while I'm cleaning my teeth."

"I'm aware I can sometimes be a bit exhausting for others to watch. I try to slow down and allow others to catch up."

People like me

Adrian Furnham – Professor of Psychology at University College London and a prolific academic psychologist who has written over 700 scientific papers and 57 books.

Lillian Gilbreth – Industrial engineer, psychologist, author and university professor. She was the first woman elected into the National Academy of Engineering – and mother to 12 children.

Ruth Lawrence – British-Israeli mathematician. She gained an O-level in Mathematics at the age of 9 and was admitted to St. Hugh's College, University of Oxford, at the age of 12.

Develop me

Coach yourself

What drives your focus on optimising your use of time?

How do you make the most of your time each day?

In what situations or contexts could you afford to relax your focus on time?

Apply yourself

In what ways do you feel others waste time? How can you help by sharing your tips, tools and technologies to speed things up?

Check in, if only quickly, with your tasks. You may tend to rush things, so make sure you are on track and have understood the instructions.

Work with others who enjoy strategic thinking or planning, so that you maximise your efficiency with their ability to cover all aspects of the task.

Watch out for yourself

Don't over-optimise every second. Your strength in maximising your time can, if overplayed, be exhausting for everyone. Learn to enjoy moments when you aren't rushing somewhere or doing something. Sometimes the best way to spend your time is in doing nothing.

Unconditionality

Understand me

I naturally accept people for who and what they are, without ever judging them. I watch and accept people with respect, as I believe that everyone is valuable in their own right. No matter what people may have done, I accept everyone the same – unconditionally.

Describe me

"I'll often defend someone's actions when other people are judging them. I believe something must have led them to behave like that."

"In life, we all make mistakes. It's important to accept people, whatever they have done. No one is perfect."

"In my view, it's important to accept someone's faults as well as their good qualities. Our experiences make us who we are."

"My friends and family often talk to me about their problems, as I don't judge their situations or what they have done. I'm trusted."

"As my door is always open (and always used), I do need to make sure my relationships are two-way sometimes."

People like me

Mata Amritanandamayi – Indian Hindu spiritual leader. She is known as the 'Hugging Saint' and widely respected for her humanitarian activities.

Jerold Bozarth – Leading practitioner of non-directive client-centred therapy. His unconditional positive regard is one of the central precepts of the approach.

Mother Teresa of Calcutta – Albanian Catholic nun. She was the founder of the Missionaries of Charity in Calcutta (now Kolkata), India, and a Nobel Peace Prize recipient for her humanitarian work.

Develop me

Coach yourself

What lies at the root of your strength in seeing the good in everyone?

In what ways do you show your appreciation and acceptance of others?

How does your appreciation and acceptance of people benefit you and other people?

Apply yourself

When decisions are being made, step in to make sure everyone is included and all views are considered in the process, especially those who can't speak up for themselves.

You see the good in people when others don't. Look to support anyone that other people have chosen to ignore and make a difference.

Speak up more in work or social settings when you feel someone is being judged. Share your knowledge and views, and in time, you may shift the mindset of those around you.

Watch out for yourself

Don't be too forgiving. Your strength in accepting people for who they are can, if overplayed, make you blind to behaviour that is unacceptable. Balance your acceptance with a willingness to be an honest friend when required. Tough love is sometimes what's needed.

Work Ethic

Understand me

I'm an extremely hard worker, putting a lot of effort and energy into my work. I enjoy putting in extra hours and I'm capable of working longer – and over a longer period of time – than most other people. I'm aware that I work much harder than others and I enjoy doing it.

Describe me

"My view is that in life you only get out what you put in. I naturally throw myself into my work."

"I always work hard, and as long as I can remember I always have. It's been instilled in me that hard work pays off."

"Whatever I am doing, I love to be busy. Even on a day off or at the weekend, I need to paint a room or transform the garden."

"I look forward to tasks where I know I am going to have to put in a lot of effort and hours. The result is so much more rewarding and satisfying."

"I do need others sometimes to remind me to spend more time with my friends and family. It's easy to let work take over."

People like me

John Henry – Figure in American folklore. He was known for his hard work on railroads and for having raced against a steam-powered hammer in a competition, and won, only to die in victory.

Marissa Mayer – Former CEO of Yahoo. She is known for her incredible stamina and work schedule, putting in 130-hour weeks at Google by sleeping under her desk.

Venus and Serena Williams – Professional tennis players. From the age of 7 they have trained tirelessly to go on to win 30 Grand Slam titles between them.

The Strengths Profile Book

Develop me

⏱ Coach yourself

What drives the strong Work Ethic in you?

When do you experience the most satisfaction from putting in long hours and hard work?

What impact does your strong Work Ethic have on you and those around you?

✓ Apply yourself

Regularly evaluate whether you are working on the right things at the right time. With the amount of effort you put in, you wouldn't want the goals to have moved and not know about it.

While you are an exceptionally strong role model to others with your hard work, let them know you don't expect the same from them. Be explicit in your communication so others don't feel lazy.

Do take time out to enjoy the success of your hard work and connect with others. No doubt you will need them on your next project!

⚠ Watch out for yourself

Know when enough is enough. Your strength in doing more than is expected of you can, if overplayed, have a negative impact on your health and relationships. Strive for a balance that meets your wider life needs, not just those of your work.

Writer

Understand me

I love to write, finding a deep fulfilment in playing with words and the joys of written language. I have a natural ability to communicate through writing. The act of writing helps me to clarify my thoughts and I write clearly and easily. I take positive pleasure in words and love to write things for others to read.

Describe me

"I love to write, about anything, at any time. I find it relaxing."

"I spend time carefully crafting my written communications. Even my text messages use the right words."

"Time seems to go so fast when I am writing. I can get lost in the message that I wanted to put across and the words just flow."

"I use the stories, challenges and experiences of people I meet as part of my writing. It helps me bring things to life."

"It's taken me a while to realise that not everyone likes to read something, some people prefer a simple call!"

People like me

Jane Austen – 19th century English novelist. She became one of the most widely read novelists in English literature, with works including *Sense and Sensibility* and *Pride and Prejudice*.

William Shakespeare – English playwright and poet. He was widely regarded as the greatest writer in the English language and is famous for such works as *Romeo and Juliet* and *Hamlet*.

Alice Walker – American novelist. She was the first black female winner of the Pulitzer Prize for Fiction and the National Book Award, both with *The Color Purple*.

Develop me

⏱ Coach yourself

What sort of writing do you enjoy most?

What was the last piece of written work that you were proud of? What was the outcome?

How does your writing ability help you achieve your daily tasks?

✓ Apply yourself

Use a variety of formats to keep your readers engaged. Well written emails and newsletters may suffice, instead of that white paper or report.

Consider your audiences. Whilst you may well prefer a thoughtful blog, they may prefer a quote or some simple bullet-point facts.

Get some feedback. What do your readers enjoy, what do you get the most 'likes' for and how do they find your use of words? Keep adding new words to your dictionary and try them out.

⚠ Watch out for yourself

Don't become a bookworm. Your strength in conveying your thoughts and ideas succinctly through writing can, if overplayed, become all consuming. Balance your love of writing with wider social communication skills and your other interests.

Part 3:

Developing and Applying Strengths

Strengths Fact

The most common **learned behaviour** in the world is

Work Ethic

To find out more about our global strengths data, visit
www.strengthsprofile.com

Strengthspotting

You know what a strength is and hopefully by now you are confident on your own strengths and what they mean for you.

In this section, we look at how you can develop these strengths even further with learning more about the strengths approach and tips to be your best self every day.

Let's start with Strengthspotting: that is identifying the things people **can do + love to do**. While our strengths assessment will give you an accurate Strengths Profile, you can also learn how to watch out for the tell-tale signs of strengths.

By becoming a strengthspotter, at work and at home, you can take the opportunity to give positive feedback. Tell the person what you saw, what strength they were using, and the impact it had. It will help encourage more of that behaviour and grow confidence as you shine a light on the value of their strengths.

To identify strengths in yourself and others, these are our top ten things to watch out for – also known as our Strengthspotting tips:

1. **Childhood memories**: What do you remember doing as a child that you still do now – but most likely even better? Strengths often have deep roots from our early lives.

2. **Energy**: What activities give you an energetic buzz when you are doing them and make you feel good? These activities are very likely calling on your strengths.

3. **Authenticity**: When do you feel most like the 'real you'? The chances are that you'll be using your strengths in some way.

4. **Ease**: See what activities come naturally to you and at which you excel – sometimes, it seems, without even trying. These will likely be your strengths.

5. **Attention**: See where you naturally pay attention. You're more likely to focus on things that are playing to your strengths.

6. **Rapid learning**: What are the things that you have picked up quickly, learning them almost effortlessly? Rapid learning often indicates an underlying strength.

7. **Motivation**: What motivates you? When you find activities that you do simply for the love of doing them, you are likely to be working from your strengths.

8. **Voice**: Monitor your tone of voice. When you notice a shift in passion, energy, or engagement, you're probably talking about a strength.

9. **Words and phrases**: Listen to the words you use. When you're saying "I love to…" or "It's just great when…", the chances are that it's a strength to which you're referring.

10. **To-do lists**: Notice the things that never make it on to your 'to-do list'. The tasks that always seem to get done often reveal an underlying strength, which means we never need to be asked twice.

Once you have mastered these tips, naturally bring them into your conversations with people. Notice these ways in your friends, children, and colleagues, and try to find the specific strength in the book that they are using.

It's the difference between "Well done, that's great" and "Well done, I can see how using your ability to naturally connect with that person so quickly really put them at ease and made a difference to how quickly they settled in".

Strengths in your context

Strengths apply to everyone. Who wouldn't want to know more about the things they are passionate about and that deliver results?

However, we all wear many hats with the different roles we have in our lives and even in our day. We've summarised some helpful ways of what this means for you in your personal and work life, and as a parent or manager.

Strengthening your personal life

Consider how your strengths complement or are different from the strengths of others in the household or your friendships. If you have similar strengths, how do they help you get things done and make decisions? Do things together that bring out these shared connections, such as a competitive game, a sci-fi movie, or learning something new.

If you have different strengths, recognise and appreciate the diversity. Point out how differences can help you see things from another point of view and find better ways of connecting. Everything doesn't always need to be put away and it doesn't always need to be left out!

What hobbies have you always wanted to take up but haven't? Your strengths may suggest it's a bad idea (you love singing, but Spotlight is a weakness) or you may realise there is no time to delay in signing on the dotted line (you've always wanted to join the Parent-Teacher Association and Organiser is a strength).

Build people's confidence in strengths by recognising and appreciating what they are good at, however small the task. It can be all too easy to be critical at home or take people for granted.

It can often be hard for good feedback to stick – we are usually looking for the negative. Help friends see what you see and appreciate in them. Be genuine and specific and let them know the positive result that their advice or action had.

Strengthening your work life

If you already enjoy what you do, you can use strengths to fine-tune your role. If you have a Strengths Profile, consider who you can delegate your energy zapping learned behaviours to (things we are good at but don't enjoy). Identify ways you can use an unrealised strength that you are passionate about developing.

If you feel your role isn't quite right for you, before considering leaving, look to make adjustments. Actively look for tasks and duties that will use your strengths more, even if they are outside of your role. Volunteer for additional responsibility that allows you to use different strengths. It's a great way to showcase strengths to people who may not have seen them in action before. What would it take to use your learned behaviours only when needed, and to explore who can support you with any critical weaknesses?

Recognise your colleagues' strengths (and weaknesses) so you know how you can support each other to be more effective. Team up for a powerful result when you share strengths and complement each other where you are different. Share your strengths with your manager and set goals and tasks according to your strengths.

Your strengths can be realised strengths (those you use often) or unrealised strengths (those that you don't use as often). Your truly greatest areas for development are in your unrealised strengths.

If you are looking to change jobs, use your Strengths Profile to give you the language of strengths in your application and interviews. Nearly half of employers are today adopting some form of strengths-based recruitment process.

Try not to overplay strengths by taking them too far. You will find tips on this under each strength in Part 2, The 60 Strengths, starting on page 21, but the key is to dial them up and down according to your need and context – not your preference!

Strengthening parents

When you see your child doing something well, stop and ask yourself if you also see the energy that would suggest it's a strength. If not, you may be at risk of ingraining a learned behaviour because you are rewarding them (praise, a pat on the back, a chocolate bar, or a trip out) for something that they do well but that isn't a strength.

Encourage them to know themselves. Talk about strengths at home. Pick up on subtle clues about their day that can open an opportunity to reinforce a strength, or to recognise things that they may simply not be so good at – and reassure them that this is OK.

At school, your children may well have learned to be well-rounded and pick subjects they do well at, rather than those they enjoy. While this will see them starting on solid ground for their future, it won't teach them that their success is likely to come from being exceptional at a few things.

When you do see that spark of greatness in your child, try planting a 'golden seed' – a kind word, a hug, reinforcement, encouragement, or positive feedback. If these golden seeds are sown in the fertile ground of a nascent strength, they could sustain your child for a lifetime.

Remember that academic success is not everything, and there are many ways to be successful in life. If your child doesn't succeed in one area, they'll likely be able to shine somewhere else. Your job as a parent is to help them explore those options and find what's right for them. Praise effort rather than attainment to help them develop a growth mindset.

Above all else, love your children for who and what they are. You created them, and they will hopefully carry your genes and your legacy into the future. Act so that you can be proud of who you are as a parent, and proud of who they are as the children you have raised.

Strengthening managers

You'll be used to looking for good performance, but now you know this simply isn't enough. If you want performance to be sustainable, and you want to create engaged and happy teams that are the envy of your peers and the pride of your own managers, identify your employees' strengths.

Get to know your own strengths. Share your own strengths stories with your team and understand how you are different or similar to each team member. Let the team know about your weaknesses, so you can allow the team's strengths to compensate for you when needed. Role model the strengths approach in your management interactions.

Help your team members to harness their strengths in delivering your team objectives and corporate strategy. Use our Manager Profile and Manager Toolkit to learn more about strengths-based management. It's full of tips on how to bring strengths more into your management conversations and daily meetings (**www.strengthsprofile.com/who/managers**).

Understand and harness the collective strengths of your team through our Team Profile. Run a team workshop so your whole team can appreciate and take responsibility for developing each other's strengths, rather than just your own. Our Team Toolkit gives you 30+ exercises to help facilitate a successful workshop.

Don't waste your organisation's money, your employees' engagement, and your own valuable time on trying to make people great in their areas of weakness. By all means, use weaknesses less to make them irrelevant, but please stop trying to make people great at their weaknesses. It won't happen and you risk doing a lot of damage along the way.

Recognise that any competency framework strives to make well-rounded individuals that churn out similar performance and attitude towards tasks at best – and usually it just ends up being dull and disengaging. Strengths on the other hand allow individuals and teams to shine to their highest potential. You get people with passion performing in roles they love.

Understand and leverage your role as a climate engineer for your team. As the manager, what you do has impact – whether you recognise it or not. As the saying goes, "When the leader sneezes, the organisation catches a cold". It's the same for you as a manager. If you sneeze, your team catches a cold. Use your climate control to create the team environment of which you can be proud.

Identify people's strengths as enablers of performance and reward them for the outcome (not for just using their strengths). In this way, you reinforce that the how matters just as much as the what and the why.

Become the super strengthspotter of your team and catch people doing things well, then share this with them. Teach yourself the Strengthspotting tips (page 144) and see what strengths you can spot in your team on an ongoing basis. Not only will you create a powerfully positive climate through that individual recognition, you'll also be much better equipped in knowing who should do what when it comes to task allocation and team working.

The Strengths Profile Model of Development

We've told you about strengths and helped you identify your own strengths. Hopefully this has got you off to a great start and you are now ready to take some action.

In our Strengths Profile Model of Development that features in the online assessment, we look at more of a holistic view of ourselves. It measures the 60 strengths mentioned in this book already, across the three areas of performance, energy, and use (how we define a strength). The results reveal your realised and unrealised strengths, learned behaviours and weaknesses, in a unique Quadrant Profile, an example of which is shown below.

We have four Strengths Profiles available: Introductory, Expert, Team and Manager. Visit **www.strengthsprofile.com** to learn more and download samples.

This holistic model gives a much more comprehensive and integrated way of understanding who we are as individual human beings. It helps us understand why we do what we do, understand the areas where we will shine and have the potential to shine, and also where we will struggle.

See below for our Model of Development which focuses on the use advice for each quadrant. By applying this advice you can focus on setting the right goals now and in the future, and asking for the right help.

In the following pages, we go on to look at how you can use the Model with your Strengths Profile results to help you become happier and more fulfilled.

If you've not taken the assessment, you can still read on to help you identify and take action in relation to each of your realised and unrealised strengths, learned behaviours and weaknesses.

Realised strengths

REALISED STRENGTHS
Strengths you use and enjoy

Perform well   Energising   Higher use

Use wisely

Here's how to be your best self through using your realised strengths wisely.

Understand your realised strengths

First and foremost, you need to really understand them. That means not confusing them with learned behaviours, or things that we enjoy but never have a chance of being really good at.

To really understand your strengths means identifying those activities at which you excel and make you feel energised. Ask yourself:

- Why do you do what you do?

- Why is it important to act in a certain way?

- What successes does acting in this way bring?

When you know this, you will then be prepared to put in the hours and effort needed for making a strength truly great. Review the coaching questions in this book for your strengths and visit the Self-aware element of the 'Be Your Best SELF' section on page 168 to start your deeper strengths discovery.

Be your own regular coach, as our strengths are constantly evolving, developing, and surprising us; after all, every situation is different.

Align strengths to goals

Strengths need to be used in context, never in isolation. There's little point in having Personalisation as a strength if you don't work with people, or Planner if there's nothing to plan. To develop your strengths to best effect, you need to be clear on how they align to what you are doing.

- What are your goals and objectives?

- What do you want to achieve now?

- What do you want to achieve in two years?

Having answered these questions, you can then start to look at how your strengths will be able to help you make progress and achieve what you want.

Combine strengths

You don't just have one or two strengths, but rather a range of strengths that you can draw on.

- What do your strengths look like in combination?

- Which combinations support what you want to achieve?

As an example, Competitive combined with Compassion looks very different to Competitive paired with Drive. Finding the right combinations of strengths can be very powerful as you double the effect of the strengths.

Using a funny situation (Humour) delivered with a compelling story (Narrator) to convince an audience on a way forward (Persuasion) could more effective than simply being funny.

Use your strengths to compensate

Use your strengths to compensate for any impact that your learned behaviours or weaknesses have. A weakness in Detail can be overcome through using a strength in Pride. A strength in Judgement can be used to compensate for a weakness in Adherence.

Any number of compensating strengths combinations exist. Think about the ones that are open to you with your unique pattern of strengths, learned behaviours and weaknesses.

Evaluate and refine

Having put together your strengths action plan, put it into practice and see how you get on.

- What's working? What isn't?

- Are you harnessing the most effective combinations of strengths to compensate for any draining learned behaviours and weaknesses?

Remember that strengths use is always a journey, never a destination.

Don't overplay strengths

Strengths overplayed can lead to declines in performance and much annoyance for others, so we need to be careful to use our strengths wisely. Pay attention to your context, making sure to use the strength to the right amount.

Strengths do not have an on/off switch, but rather a volume control: we can turn them up or turn them down as appropriate for the situation.

If you're unsure yourself, collect honest feedback from those around you to keep them appropriately used and optimally aligned to what you are striving to achieve.

You can find more of our advice on overplaying your strengths on page 164.

Unrealised strengths

Your unrealised strengths represent a depth of potential that sits within you, and from which you can draw on, as you seek to grow and develop yourself and your abilities.

In our strengths work, we often hear phrases like 'your hidden treasure box' or 'the gold at the end of your rainbow'. When you discover your unrealised strengths, it seems to make sense and stirs something in you. Use them more, blow away the cobwebs, and let them shine.

Identify your unrealised strengths

Unless you have a Strengths Profile, it may be harder to identify your unrealised strengths, because sometimes you may not know that they exist. After identifying your strengths from the 60 in this book, try rating each of them on a scale of 1-10 on use to help you consider which may be more unrealised.

You can also pay attention to things that you do for leisure. These are the things that you choose to do, so they can be an indicator of a promising or blossoming strength.

Further, think about who you admire and why you admire them. Sometimes we look up to our heroes and heroines because they do things we cannot, or improve something in themselves that resonates with us.

An unrealised strength could also be something you have used successfully before (a realised strength) but have chosen, directly or indirectly, to use less now.

Find the need/opportunity

By definition, an unrealised strength is not being used often, and this may reflect the fact that you lack the need or opportunity to use it. If so, what can you do to change this?

Of course, just trying things out can be a motivation that creates the opportunity in itself. However, you might also explore linking your unrealised strengths to tasks that need to be done at home or work. This can provide you with a safe environment to experiment with your new behaviours.

Consider opting for extra activities outside of your natural role to gain experience. What would the impact be if you dialled up an unrealised strength by just 10%? How would combining it with a realised strength help this hidden talent come through to the forefront?

Practise

If it is a new strength, you can practise using it. You are likely to experience rapid learning when you start using a strength, and this can be a very good indicator that we have accurately identified an unrealised strength in ourselves.

If so, the practice won't be onerous on you, but rather a pleasurable opportunity to master a new way of working that will serve you in many ways.

Develop

Your practice, however, can only get you so far. To really develop an unrealised strength to the full, you might also need to bring in additional learning and development.

Try both formal courses and on-the-job experience. Pay close attention to people who already display the strength far better than you do, studying them to see what you can learn and emulate from their example.

In doing so, you will never simply be making copycat reproductions of them, since you'll also be learning how the strength plays out uniquely for you, and how you can get the best from it while being at your most authentic.

Develop into a realised strength

With practice, development and use, the unrealised strength will become more realised over time. You will be using it more and becoming more successful in doing so. As this happens, you can turn your attention to where you want to go and what you do with it next.

- Can you expand the repertoire of your strength, taking on bigger or more complex activities that require you to use it?

- Can you extend it into new situations and environments, trying out new behaviours that give you the opportunity to test, explore and develop?

Evaluate

Finally, as you work your way through all these steps for developing your unrealised strengths, you should constantly be testing your ideas through your experience, the feedback of others, using the strength in practice and evaluating how you get on. Periodically return to these questions, to truly optimise your growth and development through using your unrealised strengths more.

- Did you get the results you expected?

- What have you learned along the way?

- What can you improve as you move forward with developing this strength?

Learned behaviours

LEARNED BEHAVIOURS

Things you've learned to do but may not enjoy

Perform well   De-energising   Variable use

Use when needed

Using your learned behaviours will give you performance but not energy. Consider the tasks you often get positive reinforcement from or feel a sense of achievement on a job well done – but then need a holiday to get over the project!

Learned behaviours arise through a combination of being good at something and receiving positive reinforcement. We can feel confused when we feel burned out and exhausted, as we fall into the trap of thinking that we have been playing to our strengths. As they're missing the energy component, they are not sustainable and could lead to burnout.

Learned behaviours aren't bad; after all, they are things that we do well. It's just that they are de-energising over time. To be at your best over the long-term, you need to use your learned behaviours as needed rather than relying on them all the time.

Stop doing it

What would happen if you stopped using a learned behaviour? It could have simply become ingrained and automatic. It is possible you may be able to stop without any impact on your responsibilities. If so, you'll make space to use your strengths more, with all the benefits that brings.

If this is unlikely, after all you have learned it for a helpful reason no doubt, then consider pressing the pause button for a short while to give yourself a break.

Refocus the role

Can you refocus what you do? Reorganise your activities in a way that reduces the extent to which you have to use a particular learned behaviour. In doing so you will ideally play more to your realised and unrealised strengths.

Timing: organise tasks into 'strengths sandwiches'

Can you be more mindful of how and when you complete less energising activities? Try to create a better balance by sandwiching activities that drain you between more energising activities that play to your strengths.

Don't be fooled into thinking that putting a whole day aside to tackle your year's expenses will work. Dealing with things in bite-sized chunks is better, especially when sandwiched between other tasks that will re-energise you.

Find a complementary partner

Work with someone who would be energised by taking on the things that you get drained by. In return, do something for them that they struggle with, which will help performance for both of you to be sustainable over time.

Adopt strengths-based team working

Can you reorganise how things are done using a 'team strengths' rather than 'task-led' approach? Try to reallocate tasks, objectives, or responsibilities according to what people are energised by, rather than only what they do well.

This will require an honest dialogue from everyone about whether they truly enjoy the things they may have been recognised for but weren't energised by.

Review our Strengthspotting tips on page 144 to become even more attuned to spotting energy in others.

Weaknesses

WEAKNESSES
Things you find hard and don't enjoy
Perform poorly   De-energising   Variable use
Use less

When weaknesses are used they lead to feelings of negativity, disengagement, and lack of motivation. The usual reasons are the result of some combination of our negativity bias (through evolution we naturally attend to what's wrong), poor job design (the job spec was written based on the last person who did it rather than what needs to be done), and bad management (all the above coming together through an unfortunate individual who has management responsibilities).

Over the years we have been asked why we called these aspects of the Strengths Profile 'weaknesses'. Why not 'lesser strengths' or 'areas for development'?

First, a weakness is a weakness – so let's call it that and accept it. Whilst not initially easy, accepting a weakness as such means that we can get on with dealing with it and focusing our development on our strengths. It also means that we can ask for help where we need it, and be more honest about the work and roles that we are suited for and those we are not – avoiding a lot of stress in the process.

Second, an 'area for development' should be something where you can develop to become really good, if not fantastic – and that's not ever going to be in an area of weakness.

To be clear, we aren't saying that any negative impact of weaknesses shouldn't be addressed, so as not to undermine performance. We are simply saying we shouldn't be wasting people's time and organisations' money trying to make people excel in things at which they are inherently poor.

Any development focused exclusively on weaknesses is, quite simply, wrong and ineffective. People end up feeling like failures in the process, like the good old 'presentation course' which tries to teach someone who prefers staying in the background to stand on stage.

Whilst the training could get someone to do the activity and they may even do it acceptably, they won't have slept for a week before and will be completely exhausted afterwards, hoping they never have to do it again.

We need to know what our weaknesses are, and then manage them in a way that minimises them and makes their impact irrelevant.

Fortunately, many of us have learned how to already do this – and the best performers manage to do it exceptionally well. Here is how to use your weaknesses less and minimise their impact:

Reshape the role

Can you reshape what you do? Try to reorganise what you do in a way that reduces the extent to which you have to use the weakness, ideally so that you don't have to use it at all. Do this by delegating to others – if you can – or by rearranging the way that work gets done.

Reshape your approach

Through our own research we know that Competitive is one of the most common weaknesses in the world. When the task requires you to have a winning streak, consider achieving it by using a different strength. What if you viewed the task as not being Competitive but providing a great Service so clients came back or spent more? What if it wasn't making small talk (Rapport Builder), but instead you tasked yourself with finding out more about something of interest about the person (Curiosity)?

Use strengths to compensate

Can you use or apply one or more of your strengths in such a way that your weakness is compensated for? For example, a strength in Personal Responsibility might enable a weakness in

Planner to be overcome. A strength in Resilience might enable you to overcome a weakness in Feedback.

Find a complementary partner

Try to find someone who can compensate for you and support you, someone who has a strength where you have a weakness. In return, do something for them that they struggle with and that you do well.

Adopt strengths-based team working

Try and work more using a 'team strengths' approach. Lean on your team members more by allocating tasks, objectives, or responsibilities according to the strengths of people. To be clear, this approach isn't about ridding yourself of everything you don't like in your role, but working as a team when the impact of weaknesses is critical.

Undertake development to mitigate the weakness

If none of the above are possible, can you learn to practise this weakness to a level of competence? Recognise and accept that the weakness is not something you're ever likely to do well in or be energised by.

Instead, aim to be as good as you need to be – in other words good enough, so that the weakness is minimised and no longer undermines your overall performance.

Strengths overplayed

It's important to remember it isn't the case that you should always 'use your strengths more'. Placing your (realised) strengths into overdrive without consideration of your context could be detrimental to your success. You won't win any friends this way either.

First, before using a strength more, ensure it is a strength in the first place, not just 'something you are good at'. It may make sense to do more things you perform well at, especially if you get recognition for doing them. However, it is a good job you know by now this is a learned behaviour, not a strength, and these should only be used when needed.

Second, even if you have the performance and energy, it doesn't necessarily mean it's the right time or situation to put that strength into overdrive.

Given that strengths are energising and we're good at them, we can easily be tempted into taking them too far – and overplayed strengths can lead to a decline in performance.

One example is Personal Responsibility. Imagine you love to take ownership of a task or situation and always see it through to completion. It's an excellent strength to help you succeed with your responsibilities and tasks.

You may, however, tend to volunteer for tasks that you don't need to be involved in, and delegating is not your forte, as you prefer to see something through yourself. When overplayed, you could see yourself exhausted, regretting taking on everyone else's tasks and not enabling others enough.

Eventually, over time you may lose the energy side of your Personal Responsibility, seeing it turn from a realised strength into a learned behaviour.

You can avoid this by knowing your context, audience, and need. What is it appropriate to do in the situation and context in which you find yourself? This is especially true when the context or need has changed.

We have seen many people who are great in one situation but not in another. The challenge is that because it has worked once, people think that it will work again. When it doesn't, they think they should just do it even more. Better situational judgement is essential, along with knowing how much of any given strength to use at any given time.

It's also worth considering your range of strengths for your situation. Don't just use your favourite and the one that usually works, consider instead which would be perfect for the task ahead.

We call it the 'Golden Mean of Strengths Use'. Use your judgement to call on the right strength, at the right time, using it the right amount.

While Improver will be the right strength to call on when you need to make something better, it won't be the right one to call on when you have a tight deadline. Planner and Organiser will help your project go smoothly, but Planner and Strategic Awareness will potentially future proof what you are trying to achieve.

In Part 2 of this book, in each strength's Watch Out For Yourself section, you will find more advice on how each strength could be overplayed.

Finally, remember that the Strengths Profile Model of Development advises you to use your unrealised strengths 'more'. Dialling these up is likely to showcase new talents, so go ahead, they are things you perform well at, have energy in, but use less often – and so have the opportunity to use more!

Do strengths change over time?

It was often thought that our strengths stayed with us throughout our lives – and that can be true to an extent.

We now talk about strengths being more dynamic. Over time we learn new skills, get excited about new things, and our context and situation will inevitably change regularly.

All of this means that we adapt to our surroundings. We may develop and call on different strengths to help us through challenges, job changes, new relationships, and life events. A strength that was relevant to use in one situation previously may be replaced by a strength that suits a new situation even better.

Your performance in a strength is likely to remain and we hope you continually develop and refine to make it brilliant. However, your energy and use in a strength are the ones to watch.

When the energy you once felt from a strength starts to drain away, this can often be as a result of an overplayed strength (see page 164).

Let's say you have a strength in Compassion. You love to care, really care, and others may rely on this quality in you. However, over time people come to rely on you too much and sometimes there feels like there is no escaping from people's problems.

The result could be that you would still be good at caring, it's who you are, but you may find it somewhat draining now. In the Strengths Profile, the overuse of Compassion could see your realised strength turn into a learned behaviour over time.

The good news is that once you realise this, you can soon get to work in bringing back the energy by only using it when needed. Perhaps you might rest your caring nature with others for a while and care about yourself as first priority, or only use it in certain situations with your family and friends, not in every situation.

Let's come on to the use element of a strength. You may change roles at work or take up a hobby, and it may become less relevant to use some strengths as much as you used to. These changes might result in a realised strength becoming an unrealised strength (used less), or an unrealised strength becoming a realised strength (used more).

An example here might be Organiser. You enjoy using it, it serves you well, and can be extremely useful. However, as you progress, it may be that other people take on more of this, leaving you free to explore new responsibilities.

A strength may be more useful in isolated projects or you might start to use it more at home than work. Whilst you are still good at, and enjoy using the strength, you are choosing when to call on it, thereby changing the use.

You can see how the context can change your strengths, particularly as we define strengths as being based on the combination of performance, energy, and use. It is important to recognise that strengths might not change significantly, and that changes happen over time rather than overnight.

We would recommend you retake a Strengths Profile every 12 months to keep you focused on your strengths journey. You will probably find that a few changes have taken place but that they make sense to you.

Hopefully, these will be positive changes you have been intentionally working on but if not, use the results as a wake-up call and take some action. You will also find that you have 'key' or 'signature' strengths that will stay with you always, whatever life throws at you.

Be Your Best SELF

"What next?" is the most frequently asked strengths question. By this we mean questions like "What do I do next with my Strengths Profile?", "How do I get my team to use their strengths every day?", and "How can I build a strengths-based environment at work?".

Remember that strengths is an approach, rather than a thing. So whether you are an individual or an organisation thinking about adopting a strengths-based approach, consider the journey. It's about changing yourself or the culture.

Consider what it would look like if everyone at work knew their strengths and loved what they did. What would it take to achieve this?

The SELF Model is an easy step-by-step guide to keep strengths front of mind and help you achieve your strengths journey. Your strengths aren't something to read about, resonate with, and then forget, but an approach you can apply every day. By doing so, you will not only be more successful, but also happier, more fulfilled, and able to enjoy your life more.

Within the SELF Model we've given you tips to help you apply each step, and if you visit **www.strengthsprofile.com/self** you'll find more tools and resources that we've developed for you. As an individual, you are already reading this book, which is a fantastic start, now read on to discover how you can get more from your strengths.

The Strengths Profile Book

Self-aware

Your strengths journey starts in the most obvious, but not the most practised, place. How often, in our busy lives, do we take time out and invest in ourselves? Understanding the benefits of strengths and then realising your own strengths can unlock you from having a job you 'can do' to having a job you 'love to do'.

Understand strengths

When we know what strengths can do for us, we engage with the approach and take it more seriously. Spending time on yourself could make you feel a bit indulgent, but knowing that it will help you achieve your goals and be more productive will spur you on. Consider the one area of your life you would like to improve and how your strengths can help you.

Learning how to spot strengths in yourself and others can be key to unlocking your own and others' talents. Understand how different tasks at work and at home make you feel. Some tasks, despite you being good at them, can be draining, but you may have chosen to ignore this due to your good performance.

Try to understand which tasks you undertake that leave you buzzing with excitement, and in contrast, those where you need a constant reminder to even get around to. What task was the highlight of your day? Was it the people, the change, the improvement, or the difference it will make that you loved? In contrast, what was it about the draining tasks that exhausted you? See our Strengthspotting tips on page 144.

Don't keep strengths to yourself, start dropping them into conversations and get everyone interested. Strengths brings people together as we get to share common interests and can support each other.

Discover your strengths

If you are using this book to discover your strengths, then take the time to go through all the strengths, highlighting which you think might be realised (those you use) or unrealised (those you don't use as often).

Take the time to answer the coaching questions and try at least one of the application tips. If you have completed a Strengths Profile, take time to read the descriptions and advice that follows. Highlight anything you feel applies to you and any advice that you connect with.

Visit **www.strengthsprofile.com/self** to explore further SELF resources.

Explore

Once you know more about strengths, and what your own are, you can explore them further. Take time out to discover more about what they mean for you and the journey they've already been on so you can create your development action plan.

Coach yourself

Even if you have a coach, you can always employ yourself for additional homework. Use the Coach Yourself sections in Part 2 to understand where you can develop your strengths further.

What do your strengths mean to you? They are more than a word or description, they are unique to you. Consider how you use them, which ones you've learned, and which ones you've always had. Which ones would you be lost without? Which are you most proud of? Start each day considering your strengths and how they may show up today with your tasks ahead.

Consider how your strengths are serving you now in your life. Is there a chance you could be overplaying any? What is the impact of that on you and others?

You can also use The Strengths Profile Model of Development (page 151) to create an action plan of what to do in each quadrant. Which realised strengths will you use wisely? Which unrealised strengths will you use more? If you have a Strengths Profile you can also ask which learned behaviours you should use only when needed, and which weaknesses you can use less?

Share your strengths

Consider who it would be helpful to share them with. Perhaps your manager, or project or team members you work with closely. Help them to understand the strengths you would like to use more, and perhaps anything you would like to use less of. This will start them thinking on how they can align more of your strengths in projects or tasks.

Create a poster of your strengths and what you want to be known for in your role. Connect with your values and share what's important to you.

Share your Strengths Profile at home too, so you can encourage the positive culture at the dinner table and over homework! Challenge everyone to think of one strength they used that day.

You can visit **www.strengthsprofile.com/self** to explore further SELF resources.

Launch

High performers use their strengths 70% of the time so it's time to work on making your strengths count, now that you've explored them in depth. Start aligning your strengths to goals and revealing your unrealised strengths.

Love what you do

Align your personal or work goals with your strengths. You may find yourself on automatic pilot when it comes to taking action, but review whether using this approach is the best one. Look at the wide range of strengths you have, consider the task and the challenges you face, and ignite the right strength, not just your preferred strength.

Think about the relationships you might need to build, and the resources and people you will need to make this happen. For example, you could align your Personal Responsibility strength to ensure you take ownership of the task and see it through, or you could use your Enabler strength and adopt a teaching style instead.

We all know someone who just seems to love their job. At Capp, we've taken much pleasure (and embarrassed our children) in telling strangers how happy they seem in their work and then watching them smile as they tell you why.

Remember, we aren't telling you to never do anything you don't like, but to make conscious decisions about what you do, how you do it, when you do it, and who you do it with.

Tip the scales in favour of your strengths. Allow short periods of time to recover when you can't use your strengths. Use combinations of your strengths to be more effective. Take responsibility for finding new ways to use your strengths outside of your usual activities. Say yes more to the unknown in the areas of your strengths.

Strengths conversations

Working on the right things, at the right time, in the right way is essential for success. Prepare for your review conversations with your manager in advance by sharing which strengths you've used to deliver your tasks, thereby showcasing your strengths in action.

As you work together to set future goals for the year ahead, make sure you set them based on your strengths, not weaknesses. Share the unrealised strengths you've identified that you are most passionate about using more. Leave the meeting feeling excited about your future projects and tasks rather than just 'OK' about them.

Release the hidden talent of your unrealised strengths by sharing them with others more. They may not know they even exist for you, as you aren't using them often. What would it look like if you were 10% more creative, or 20% more detail-focused in your tasks at home or work? Which realised strengths (the ones we are already using) could help you out of our comfort zone when using these?

Ask for feedback from others to help you understand the impact of your strengths on those around you. What do they value most in you? Again, don't forget to ask at home too! Ask people to share any strengths they may see you overplay sometimes and any impact of this.

Give yourself some feedback too. Make a chart of three of your biggest achievements. Identify which strengths served you in delivering the successful outcome and how you got there.

You can visit **www.strengthsprofile.com/self** to explore additional SELF resources.

Flourish

The final step is to continue mastering the journey of strengths to help you have a meaningful, successful, and happy life. Learn the fine art of recognising what to work on when and which strength will deliver you the best result.

Your future

Don't be tempted to be a good 'all-rounder' or dial up all your strengths. Consider your 'strengths brand', that is, the strengths where if someone took them away you would feel like you've lost an irreplaceable friend. These are the ones you are likely to make a difference in, so continually look for roles, projects, and hobbies that involve these strengths.

Consider what you want to be known for in your current and future roles. What do you want friends and family to call you up for? When you retire, what will you have achieved that makes you proud? As you make decisions daily, consider your strengths brand and legacy, and the impact you want to have. Develop these strengths even further. Be the one to go to for all things involving these strengths.

Also, remember that strengths change over time according to your context (see page 166). We live in a world that's forever changing, so your goals might need to change or how you get there may need to be reviewed. You may need to use different strengths to support the task or to negotiate with a change in stakeholder. Consider what weaknesses you may need to compensate for when you review your goals. We all have weaknesses, but the trick is to use them less and work with others to achieve your goals.

Strengthening others

Your colleagues, friends, and family will all be playing to their strengths, whether they know it or not. Use your new Strengthspotting skills (page 144) to spot the strengths in their actions.

Appreciating not only your own but also strengths in others will go a long way to developing a strengths culture around you. Consider how these strengths complement your own and whether you have similar or different strengths.

Come up with a couple of ways you can work better together and help each other. Champion your areas of strengths, while acknowledging that this behaviour may seem different to the rest of the team. When you have common strengths, come together and set powerful goals that truly make a difference.

Visit **www.strengthsprofile.com/who/managers** if you are a manager looking for tools and Profiles to support your strengths-based management. Use the Team Profile to learn more about the collective strengths of your teams.

Celebrate your success!

The final part of the process is to write down your successes and celebrate! Consider your top seven strengths and list how each one has helped you achieve your tasks and projects at work. Highlight how they support your relationships and help you adapt to new situations.

By keeping a record, you can start to build a picture of the strengths you keep coming back to and enjoy using more. This will build confidence in your strengths use and set the path for further strengths development.

Turn up to life every day, not only wanting to be your authentic best self, but knowing how to get there.

Visit **www.strengthsprofile.com/self** for a range of toolkits to help you embed strengths into your daily working life and to explore further SELF resources.

Strengths in summary – 8 easy steps for success

We've told you a lot about strengths; what a strength is, why they're important, and how to develop them. Here's a quick recap of the most important things to remember:

1. A strength is something you perform well and have energy in.

2. Knowing and using your strengths will allow you to be your authentic best self.

3. Start Strengthspotting in all areas of your life. Note the things that give you a buzz and you look forward to, and the things you would rather someone else did. Spot strengths in others too!

4. Strengths use is a journey where you embrace a mindset change. It requires daily attention from you but like most things in life, you get out what you put in.

5. Pay attention to which strengths are realised (used often) and which are unrealised (used less often). Use the realised strengths wisely and use the unrealised strengths more.

6. If you are good at something, without the energy, this is a learned behaviour, not a strength. Only use learned behaviours when you need to, so that you avoid burnout.

7. Don't ever try to become great at your weaknesses. You never will. Instead, minimise them by using your strengths to compensate.

8. Use the tips in our SELF Model on page 168 and at **www.strengthsprofile.com/self** to keep your strengths front of mind.

Part 4:

Strengths Science and Other References

Strengths Fact

The least common realised strength in the world is

Adherence

To find out more about our global strengths data, visit
www.strengthsprofile.com

The strengths science

Many of us will be familiar with the adage 'play to your strengths'. The great news is that research has provided the scientific underpinnings for why this matters and the benefits that using your strengths brings. We use the strengths approach across all our work at Capp to help organisations assess, recruit, and develop their people using their strengths. Here's why they keep coming back to strengths.

People who use their strengths more:

1. Are happier

2. Are more confident

3. Have higher levels of self-esteem

4. Have higher levels of energy and vitality

5. Experience less stress

6. Are more resilient

7. Are more likely to achieve their goals

8. Perform better at work

9. Are more engaged at work

10. Are more effective at developing themselves and growing as individuals.

When Capp started over a decade ago, we found we needed to spend time convincing decision makers of the benefits using the strengths approach would provide. Now, with over 20 years of research, people are invested in strengths and are more interested in how it will work for them – and when can they get started.

We are data geeks at Capp and continue to collect data from all our work, so we get to see how strengths work on the ground too. Here's a summary of what our data has shown in the four areas where our reports are used.

Individuals report:

- Increased awareness of their strengths and ability to focus on these strengths, rather than focusing just on their weaknesses.

- A deeper appreciation for their strengths, an awareness of where their learned behaviours could be blocking their potential, a respect for their weaknesses, and excitement for how they might start to use their unrealised strengths more often.

- Ability to make positive personal development changes as a result of workshops.

Teams report:

- A greater understanding in how to use their strengths to be more effective at work.

- Understanding the strengths and weaknesses of their colleagues as a result of strengths development.

- Appreciating their colleagues more as a result of strengths workshops.

- Knowing how to use their strengths to be more effective at work.

Managers report:

- Deeper insights into those they are coaching and an enhanced ability to support people in achieving and unleashing their potential.

- Feeling confident in identifying strengths in themselves and their team members.

- Knowing how to manage others based on their strengths, learned behaviours, and weaknesses.

- A positive impact on workplace diversity.

Organisations report:

- Strengths language being used to support teams across daily tasks.

- Improved communications within teams through more efficient and consistent dialogue.

- Teams now delegating more around strengths, and recruiting around gaps that have been identified during workshops.

- Better ways of working and more momentum in achieving individual and team goals.

- Seeing a change in behaviour and a drive to continue their improvements, knowing they can track their progress through re-taking Strengths Profile.

Scientific sources

Here is the original scientific source material in which the 10 benefits of strengths are shown:

1. People who use their strengths more are happier:

In a study with 214 university students, Govindji & Linley (2007) showed that people who used their strengths more reported higher levels of subjective wellbeing (i.e., happiness) and psychological wellbeing (i.e., fulfilment). Similarly, Proctor, Maltby, & Linley (2009) reported similar findings with a study of 135 university students. Seligman, Steen, Park, & Peterson (2005) found that people who used their strengths in a new and different way every day reported higher levels of happiness and lower levels of depression, and this lasted over time. Minhas (2010) showed that people who developed their realised or unrealised strengths reported higher levels of happiness and wellbeing over a four-week period. Park, Peterson, & Seligman (2004) found that people who reported higher levels of character strengths also reported higher levels of life satisfaction, especially for so-called 'strengths of the heart'.

2. People who use their strengths more are more confident:

Govindji & Linley (2007) found that people who used their strengths more reported higher levels of self-efficacy, which is a scientific conception of confidence – the belief that we are capable of achieving the things we want to achieve. This finding was replicated by Proctor, Maltby, & Linley (2009) in a study with 135 university students.

3. People who use their strengths more have higher levels of self-esteem:

Minhas (2010) found that people who developed their realised or unrealised strengths reported increases in self-esteem over a four-week period. Govindji & Linley (2007) reported that people who used their strengths more reported higher levels of self-esteem. In a study with 135 university students, Proctor, Maltby, & Linley (2009) found that strengths use was associated with higher levels of self-esteem.

4. People who use their strengths more have higher levels of energy and vitality:

In a study with 214 university students, Govindji & Linley (2007) found that strengths use was associated with higher levels of psychological vitality, that is, having feelings of positive energy and buzz.

5. People who use their strengths more experience less stress:

Over a six-month period with a community sample of 207 people, those people who used their strengths more reported lower levels of stress. This was the case at both the baseline period, where strengths use was associated with less stress, and over the three-month and six-month follow ups, where higher strengths use predicted lower stress over time (Wood, Linley, Maltby, Kashdan, & Hurling, 2011).

6. People who use their strengths more are more resilient:

Analysis of the Ego Resiliency Scale with Strengths Profile showed that strengths use is associated with higher levels of resilience for 50 of the 60 Strengths Profile strengths (Capp, 2018). The two highest correlations were with Resilience (as you might expect) and Adventure, which suggests that stretching yourself outside of your comfort zone can be a way to build your resilience. The ten strengths where higher strengths use was not significantly associated with higher resilience were Adherence, Competitive, Detail, Humour, Organiser, Planner, Prevention, Time Optimiser, Work Ethic and Writer.

7. People who use their strengths more are more likely to achieve their goals:

Linley, Nielsen, Wood, Gillett, & Biswas-Diener (2010) showed that people who used their strengths in striving to achieve their goals were far more likely to achieve those goals. When they achieved their goals, they satisfied their psychological needs and were happier and more fulfilled as a result.

8. People who use their strengths more perform better at work:

In a study of 19,187 employees from 34 organisations across seven industries and 29 countries, the Corporate Leadership Council (2002) found that when managers emphasised performance strengths, performance was 36.4% higher, and when they emphasised personality strengths, performance was 21.3% higher. In contrast, emphasising weaknesses led to a 26.8% decline for performance weaknesses and a 5.5% decline for personality weaknesses. The conclusions from our own work with Norwich Union showed that people working from their strengths perform better and stay with the company longer (Stefanyszyn, 2007).

9. People who use their strengths more are more engaged at work:

The opportunity to do what you do best each day, that is, using our strengths, is a core predictor of workplace engagement, which in turn is a core predictor of a range of business outcomes (Harter, Schmidt, & Hayes, 2002). Similarly, Minhas (2010) found that work engagement increased when people developed either their realised or unrealised strengths.

10. People who use their strengths more are more effective at developing themselves and growing as individuals:

When focusing on self-development, people improve faster on areas where they are already strong than they do in areas where they are weak, contrary to some popular perceptions that focusing on weakness development brings the greatest return (Sheldon, Kasser, Smith, & Share, 2002). Case study evidence from our own work on leadership development with BAE Systems showed that business leaders who focused on developing themselves and their teams on the basis of their strengths were more effective and successful (Smedley, 2007).

References

Capp (2018). *Technical manual and statistical properties for Strengths Profile*. Capp Press, Birmingham, UK.

Corporate Leadership Council (2002). *Performance management survey*. Washington, DC.

Govindji, R., & Linley, P. A. (2007). Strengths use, self-concordance and well-being: Implications for strengths coaching and coaching psychologists. *International Coaching Psychology Review*, 2 (2), 143-153.

Harter, J. K., Schmidt, F. L., & Hayes, T. L. (2002). Business-unit-level relationship between employee satisfaction, employee engagement, and business outcomes: A meta-analysis. *Journal of Applied Psychology*, 87, 268-279.

Linley, P. A., Nielsen, K. M., Wood, A. M., Gillett, R., & Biswas-Diener, R. (2010). Using signature strengths in pursuit of goals: Effects on goal progress, need satisfaction, and well-being, and implications for coaching psychologists. *International Coaching Psychology Review*, 5 (1), 8-17.

Minhas, G. (2010). Developing realised and unrealised strengths: Implications for engagement, self-esteem, life satisfaction and well-being. *Assessment and Development Matters*, 2 (1), Spring 2010.

Park, N., Peterson, C., & Seligman, M. E. P. (2004). Strengths of character and well-being. *Journal of Social and Clinical Psychology*, 23, 603-619.

Proctor, C., Maltby, J., & Linley, P. A. (2009) Strengths use as a predictor of well-being and health-related quality of life. *Journal of Happiness Studies*, 10, 583-630.

Seligman, M. E. P., Steen, T. A., Park, N., & Peterson, C. (2005). Positive psychology progress: Empirical validation of interventions. *American Psychologist*, 60, 410-421.

Sheldon, K. M., Kasser, T., Smith, K., & Share, T. (2002). Personal goals and psychological growth: Testing an intervention to enhance goal-attainment and personality integration. *Journal of Personality*, 70, 5-31.

Smedley, T. (2007). The powers that BAE. *People Management,* November, 40-42.

Stefanyszyn, K. (2007). Norwich Union changes focus from competencies to strengths. *Strategic HR Review*, 7, 10-11.

Wood, A. M., Linley, P. A., Maltby, J., Kashdan, T. B., & Hurling, R. (2011). Using personal and psychological strengths leads to increases in well-being over time: A longitudinal study and the development of the strengths use questionnaire. *Personality and Individual Differences*, 50, 15-19.

Strengths Profile symbols

"A picture is worth a thousand words" – Anon.

Throughout our history, the symbol has been used as a shared communication medium which transcends language, history, and culture. Symbols speak to the deeper truth of something that is not easily rendered in words. They are as old as humankind itself.

In the modern age, symbols continue to be all around us. We recognise them as the badges and insignia of group membership – whether sports teams, political parties, or other groups; road user information; or corporate brands and logos. Media advertising is replete with symbols, as marketers use symbolic associations in the effort to position their brands and products in our minds alongside the attributes created by the symbols.

Generally speaking, symbols are used to emphasise the positive rather than the negative: virtue not vice; hope not despair; strength not weakness. It is only fitting, therefore, that we have developed a strengths symbology for Strengths Profile, to honour the wisdom of the ages in creating a deeper understanding of, and resonance with, human strengths.

A symbology may refer to the study of the symbols, the use of the symbols, or the symbols themselves collectively. Our strengths symbology is all three, since it is concerned with understanding how the symbols represent the different strengths, how they are used, and the symbols collectively.

We now introduce you to the symbols that we have chosen to represent each of the 60 strengths in Strengths Profile.

Symbols bibliography

Cooper, J. C. (1979). *An illustrated encyclopaedia of traditional symbols.* London: Thames & Hudson.

Fontana, D. (1997). *The secret language of symbols: A visual key to symbols and their meanings.* London: Piatkus.

Tresidder, J. (2003). *1001 symbols: The illustrated key to the world of symbols.* London: Duncan Baird Publishers.

Strengths Profile symbols

 Action — The clapperboard is used in film making to highlight the 'Action' of the famous movie-making phrase "Lights, Camera, Action!"

 Adaptable — People strong in Adaptable see life as a jigsaw puzzle and are always looking for the best fit of what will go where.

 Adherence — The tick is used to represent people ticking off everything they are supposed to do.

 Adventure — The mountains indicate the risk and stretch involved in climbing them, just like those with the strength of Adventure.

 Authenticity — The envelope seal has been used throughout the ages to show that important documents were the authentic originals, not a copy.

 Bounceback — The coiled spring represents how people with Bounceback use setbacks as a springboard to go on and do even better.

 Catalyst — Catalysts make things happen, and in this strengths symbol, the match provides the spark for things to start.

Centred — The dot at the centre is one of the oldest symbols in symbology and was often taken to represent the sun.

 Change Agent — The Greek symbol delta, here represented by a triangle, is a universal symbol for change.

 Compassion — The two hearts represent that people strong in Compassion care about others.

 Competitive — The trophy symbolises victory, which is what everyone with a Competitive strength will be striving for – to win.

 Connector — People strong in Connector are always linking people they know with other people.

 Counterpoint — Like this fish swimming against the flow, people with Counterpoint will always bring a different perspective.

 Courage — The medal awarded for bravery represents Courage throughout many histories and cultures.

Creativity — The artist's palette and paint brush are the archetypal modern symbol for Creativity, but still represent only one of the ways in which to be creative.

Curiosity

Curiosity is all about asking questions, as this strengths symbol suggests.

 Detail

The strength of Detail is about looking into the minutiae, which this magnifying glass is used to convey.

 Drive

People strong in Drive have a distinct energy about them, captured here by the lightning bolt.

 Emotional Awareness

The thermometer within the heart symbolises how people strong in Emotional Awareness are sensitive to the needs and emotions of others.

 Empathic

A hand on the heart symbolises when people are connected through their shared understanding of what the other person is feeling.

 Enabler

The seed grows in this person's hand, symbolising their role in creating the conditions for other people to learn how to grow and develop.

 Equality

The rule is used to measure, and in the case of the person strong in Equality, to measure and ensure that all receive equal parts.

Esteem Builder Esteem Builders are amazing at unlocking the energy and shine that lies within people, like the key unlocking the sun.

Explainer

They might not always need a presentation and chart, but these symbols are typical of the tools of an Explainer.

 Feedback

Feedback is a two-way process, so these arrows show the flow of dialogue through Feedback.

 Gratitude

Flowers can be a wonderful way to say thank you and show appreciation, so they became the Gratitude strengths symbol.

 Growth

The acorn is an archetypal symbol of Growth and development, since from small acorns large oak trees grow.

 Humility

The humble bumble bee works only to serve his or her queen, and so becomes our strengths symbol for Humility.

 Humour

The laughing face is a universal symbol for Humour, and so we use it here as the strengths symbol.

 Improver

People strong in Improver always want to make things better and sharper, symbolised here by the pencil sharpener.

 Incubator

The thought bubble shows where Incubators spend their time thinking things through as they ponder and reflect.

Innovation — Represented here by chemical experimentation, the symbol for Innovation represents trying things out in different and original ways.

 Judgement — To ensure the right decision, people strong in Judgement will weigh the evidence and options on all sides, as these scales show.

 Legacy — People strong in Legacy want to create things that will outlast them, symbolised here by the longevity of the tree.

 Listener — The human ear is an archetypal symbol for listening.

 Mission — This rocket ship is shooting for the stars and symbolises how people strong in Mission will always be heading straight for what is important to them.

 Moral Compass — The compass here helps people to guide their decisions towards the true north of what is the ethical and right thing to do.

 Narrator — The story book symbolises what the Narrator loves to do – tell stories!

 Optimism — Is the glass half-full or half-empty? This well-recognised way of asking whether someone is an optimist or a pessimist is used here as the strengths symbol for Optimism.

Organiser — People strong in Organiser will have a place for everything, as the neat arrangement of this bookshelf suggests.

 Persistence — Like the tortoise who won his race against the hare, people strong in Persistence will just keep going until they get to the finish line.

 Personal Responsibility — The hand raised shows how people strong in Personal Responsibility love to take ownership and volunteer to see things through.

 Personalisation — The fingerprint symbolises that people strong in Personalisation are acutely interested in your uniqueness.

 Persuasion — The lyre is renowned throughout mythology as playing the sweet music that allows people to bring others around to their way of thinking.

 Planner — Diaries and calendars are a very good way of knowing what you are going to be doing and when, as this strengths symbol conveys.

 Prevention — The lighthouse is well-recognised for its role in preventing disaster by warning ships to steer clear of the rocks.

 Pride — The '100% Quality Assured' stamp conveys that people with this strength will always strive to produce work that is of the highest quality.

Rapport Builder People strong in Rapport Builder will always make time to stop and say hello.

 Relationship Deepener The diamond represents a diamond wedding anniversary, achieved only after 60 years of marriage.

 Resilience The shield symbolises the strength of Resilience, and how it enables people to keep challenges, setbacks and disappointments at bay.

 Resolver The Swiss Army knife seems to have a function for every situation, and so is used here to symbolise the strength of Resolver.

 Self-awareness The hand mirror is used to symbolise the strength of Self-awareness, whereby people know themselves well, understanding their emotions and motivations.

 Self-belief The cloud showcasing achievement represents confidence in our future success, as found in those with Self-belief.

 Service The dinner cover, or cloche, represents a waiter renowned for their meticulous Service.

 Spotlight The Spotlight is what is sought by people with this strength, so the strengths symbol provides it for them.

Strategic Awareness

Always looking out over the horizon to see what might be coming next, the telescope symbolises Strategic Awareness.

 Time Optimiser

The clock symbolises time, and this is the unique focus of the Time Optimiser; how to make the most of whatever time is available in whatever situation.

 Unconditionality

For people strong in Unconditionality, everyone is welcome, as symbolised by this welcome mat.

 Work Ethic

The ox is universally revered for its capacity for work, and so is used here as the strengths symbol for Work Ethic.

 Writer

People strong in Writer love to write, as conveyed by this pen and heart symbol.

About the authors

Dr. Alex Linley is a world authority on positive psychology and its applications, particularly strengths approaches. He is the Founder and CEO of Capp, where he leads the company purpose of *Strengthening the World* and vision of *Matching the world to their perfect job*. In his former academic career, Alex has written, co-written, or edited more than 130 research papers and book chapters, and eight books, including *Positive Psychology in Practice* (Wiley, 2004), *Average to A+: Realising Strengths in Yourself and Others* (Capp Press, 2008), and the *Oxford Handbook of Positive Psychology and Work* (Oxford University Press, 2009), all of which he now appreciates as a result of the combination of his Legacy and Writer strengths. As well as working on strengths, Alex listens to The Cure, supports Nottingham Forest Football Club and plays with the family dachshunds, Buddy and Dash. Alex lives in the West Midlands with his wife and four children.

Trudy Bateman is an expert in strengths and their applications and as Head of Strengths Profile is responsible for implementing the successful product strategy and delivery of the tool. Having been with Capp since 2009, she has delivered thousands of strengths solutions through coaching, facilitating, and consulting. Trudy now applies her expertise and top strength of Legacy to deliver her passion in helping people and organisations to be their best. This focuses on the development of accessible tools to build strengths-based cultures and lives that are sustaining and rewarding. Trudy is a key speaker and resident expert in strengths and their applications. Trudy lives in Warwickshire with her husband, two children and two dogs, where she loves to overplay her Humour strength.

Other books by the authors

Positive Psychology in Practice

P. Alex Linley & Stephen Joseph (Eds.) (Wiley, 2004)

Positive Therapy: A Meta-Theory for Positive Psychological Practice

Stephen Joseph & P. Alex Linley (Taylor & Francis, 2006)

Average to A+: Realising Strengths in Yourself and Others

Alex Linley (Capp Press, 2008)

Trauma, Recovery and Growth: Positive Psychological Perspectives on Posttraumatic Stress

Stephen Joseph & P. Alex Linley (Eds.) (Wiley, 2008)

Oxford Handbook of Positive Psychology and Work

P. Alex Linley, Susan Harrington & Nicola Garcea (Eds.) (Oxford University Press, 2010)

The Strengths Book: Be Confident, Be Successful and Enjoy Better Relationships by Realising the Best of You (1st ed.)

Alex Linley, Janet Willars & Robert Biswas-Diener (Capp Press, 2010)

Happiness and Well-being (Critical Concepts in Psychology)

Felicia A. Huppert & P. Alex Linley (Eds.) (Routledge, 2011)

Research, Applications, and Interventions for Children and Adolescents: A Positive Psychology Perspective

Carmel Proctor & P. Alex Linley (Eds.) (Springer, 2013)

Where next?

STRENGTHS·PROFILE

Complete your Strengths Profile online at **www.strengthsprofile.com**

Already have a Strengths Profile?

Upgrade from an Introductory Profile to our Expert Profile to reveal all 60 strengths across your realised and unrealised strengths, learned behaviours and weaknesses.

SELF

View our SELF model resources and go on the step-by-step strengths journey with your Profile.

Coaches

Are you a coach and want to deepen your knowledge of strengths? Strengthen yourself, your coachees and your teams with accreditations and toolkits:

www.strengthsprofile.com/who/coaches

Managers

Are you a manager and want to strengthen your people and team? Find out how with our practical Manager Profile and Toolkit:

www.strengthsprofile.com/who/managers

Strengths Profile was developed by Capp.

To find out more about Capp's assessment, development and transformation solutions, explore **www.capp.co**

Printed in Great Britain
by Amazon